ME FOR MYSELF

When nothing makes sense

ME FOR MYSELF

When nothing makes sense

ABHISHEK AGGARWAL

I am not a professional writer or a literature graduate, so please forgive me if my words feel unconventional or differ from what you might expect in a typical book.

This book is a reflection of my personal journey through unhappiness, pain, and suffering toward discovering a deeper connection with God. I do not claim to know everything; in fact, I believe no one does. But I do believe we can all uncover insights that make life a little less heavy, a little less painful, and a little more peaceful. I have experienced some of this myself, and with this book, I hope to share that possibility with you.

I have tried to explore philosophy and spirituality in simple, relatable language, using modern-day examples to bring timeless ideas to life. I have also intentionally avoided excessive Sanskrit terms or complex philosophical jargon so that the focus remains on the essence of these concepts rather than the vocabulary.

While I am grateful to many people and experiences in my life, my deepest thanks go to my pain, my suffering, and my unhappiness. They were my greatest teachers, guiding me toward God and inspiring this book.

'Read, Understand & Question'

CONTENTS

INTRODUCTION

Humanity has created a world filled with problems and information, and we are suffering as a result. Every day, we create new problems for ourselves and try to solve them with the information we have. There is no doubt that this is taking us forward as a civilisation, but the question remains: how is it taking us forward? Is it through suffering or happiness, through contentment or desire, through love or hate? Moving forward is essential, but so is *how* we do that.

If we focus too much on reaching our destination, our journey becomes tiresome, and life is that journey. Life is the journey from where we start to where we end. Just like any journey, life is supposed to be beautiful and fun. However, every journey has its bumps. Sometimes we encounter roadwork in progress, or we have to stop for refuelling. We observe both the beautiful mountains and the accidents that have occurred while trying to reach our destination.

In this journey of life, we sometimes find ourselves confused and lost. Unfortunately, for this particular journey called life, we cannot use Google or Apple Maps to get directions. To find the direction in life, we seek help from our teachers, parents, gurus, priests, monks, religious scriptures, AI and more.

To understand this journey, we must look carefully around us, and when we do, we will see that there are two worlds: the social world and the spiritual world. The social world is like the land on which we stand, and the spiritual world is the space around us. The social world encompasses our daily lives and activities, including cooking dinner, going shopping, working, raising a family, and meeting friends and family. The spiritual world, on the other hand, includes happiness, joy, contentment, peace, anger, hate, jealousy, pain, suffering and more. To summarise, the social world encompasses our daily activities, such as going to work or caring for our families, while the spiritual world is how we go about doing it. Do we go to work with happiness and joy, or do we dread it? Do we feel content with what we have, or do we desire more? The social is what we do, and the spiritual is how we do it.

For most of us, the social world is not a problem because we are trained to deal with it. From a very young age, we are taught the skills required. Our entire education is based on the social world. However, the same cannot be said for the spiritual world, even though much information and guidance are available on it.

The problem arises when we look for an answer, a solution or guidance. Unlike our social world, our spiritual world lacks authorities to monitor the credibility and integrity of its workers. We are unsure of what to believe or whom to trust. Every guru teaches something different, every religion offers its own perspective, and each priest adheres to a set of beliefs. The guidance and direction we receive often lack credibility and are overwhelming in their abundance, making it difficult to determine whether they will truly assist us on our journey.

So what should we do as individuals and as humanity?
As humanity, we should see the spiritual world holistically,
rather than from a single point of view; and as individuals,
our best hope is to put our faith in ourselves. To look within
and understand what's there, and use that insight to guide the
journey. To look inwards and not outwards, to be for oneself.

PART 1:

TROUBLE & ADVICE

The world is full of advice. The real question is: should you take it? Start by asking yourself these questions.

Do you know how an astronaut feels when he looks at Earth from space?

Do you know what it feels like to stand on the summit of Mount Everest?

Do you know what it's like to swim between sharks?

You don't. Only someone who has actually been there can tell you.

So how could you describe the feeling of diving with sharks if you'd never dived with them? What advice could you give to an astronaut if you'd never left the Earth? Yet everywhere you look, people who haven't lived your life are telling you how to live it.

Look at the preachers, the self-styled gurus, the so-called saints. Many of them haven't been married, haven't raised children, and aren't the ones sitting through hospital halls or paying their parents' medical bills. Those who did marry, often ended up walking away from their marriages.

They haven't been in your shoes. So you must ask? How do they claim to know what you need?

It's like deciding to climb Everest, hiking up to the base camp, turning back after a few kilometres and then writing a manual titled 'How to Climb Everest'. The instructions sound noble and convincing. But are they really helpful?

Here's a simple truth: the only advice that will genuinely help you is the advice from someone who has walked a path like yours. If you look closely and carefully, you will realise something. Who, in the end, is in your shoes? You are. Not your parents, not your partner, not your children, and certainly not every tidy-tongued guru you meet. Only you can advise yourself. This may sound confusing at first, but as we explore further, it will become clearer.

So what do we do? Whom do we turn to when we're in trouble? Before we answer that, understand this—there are two kinds of trouble: internal and external.

THE FIRST STEP

Internal & External Troubles

Internal troubles refer to those that originate from within. For example, should I do this or that? Should I leave this or not? Should I choose this, or should I choose that? Making choices can be a complex internal trouble. There are simple troubles as well. Hurt is one of them. It is most commonly noticed at a young age and in old age.

When you are young, you tend to fall in love with someone, and sometimes the other person doesn't feel the same way. You feel hurt inside, and you can't do anything about it. You continue to feel hurt inside until you find someone else or until you get busy and forget about the pain. Hurt is also very commonly noticed in old age. As you grow older, you tend to start expecting more from society and family members. The most unique thing about expectation is that it can never be fulfilled—it is what our minds create to make us feel better. However, expectations, whether realistic or not, can cause hurt. People in their last days are very grumpy, angry, and frustrated. Why? Because they are hurt, as their expectations from life and people are not fulfilled.

Now, this does not mean people in their midlife don't get hurt. They do, a lot. Probably more than people in their young and old age. However, it gets overshadowed by their responsibilities and dreams. They are told to swallow their pain and keep moving forward. Haven't you seen the motivational videos on social media? I have seen a lot of them, and most of them go something like this: Get up!, Stop Crying!, No one Cares!, Start working!, Be successful!, Don't be a slave!, Make this world come to you! You must really think about it. What are these motivational speakers or videos trying to tell you? They are giving you quick fixes, so you keep running instead of fixing the issue. Ask yourself this question: if you permanently feel better after watching their videos, will you see them again? Or watch more of their videos? Probably not. It's fascinating to see what a great business this is.

Moving on to the second type of problem, namely, external problems. They are simple problems and easy to understand. For example, you forgot to file your taxes, and now the government has sent you a letter stating that you need to pay them soon or face jail time. Now, many people panic, start calling their friends and family, discuss it for days, and stress about it. However, in this situation, one could remain calm and go to the nearest accountant, who will fix it in an hour.

Let's look at another example of an extreme external problem: imagine you are a new parent with a mountain of expenses, and you're the only one with a job. The company you work for decides to close the division you work in, and you're made redundant—a complicated external problem. You have a partner and a newborn who require a lot of care, and nappies are not cheap these days, right? You have a mortgage, a partner, and a child to support. What do you do? A big external problem. However, if you think calmly and consider your options, you might find a solution. You can ask your parents for help, maybe reach out for government support, or start doing a job that doesn't require much skill to get by.

However, the same cannot be said for internal problems. The difference is that one can only be solved internally, and the other can only be solved externally. You cannot get a job by thinking about what life is. And you cannot resolve an ethical dilemma by buying an expensive car.

Most people face external troubles for most of their lives. They develop a better understanding of these troubles, which is the key to solving them. On the contrary, people face internal troubles at least once in their lifetime, if not more often. You may say, if we only face it once or twice, we can simply ignore it. I say the opposite. Because when you face them less often, you are least prepared for them. Just like soldiers go to war only a few times in their entire career, but are trained continuously to be prepared. Similarly, you must be ready to address internal troubles.

So, how do you prepare yourself for such troubles? The answer is by understanding them. Internal troubles are the most difficult to resolve. Why? Because it is a fight within. How does one fight with oneself? When I say 'oneself', I mean our beliefs and our personality.

Let's look at some common examples of internal troubles. A prevalent example is when a married man's wife and mother don't see eye to eye. What is the right thing to do? The man loves his wife and wants to do everything to make her happy, but it's his mother who gave birth to him and played a significant role in shaping who he is. If the wife and mother fought, whose side should he take? Now, this may sound like a minor internal trouble to women, but I suggest asking a man.

Another example of internal trouble is when a wife loves her husband very much but hates it when he drinks. She tries to express her concerns on multiple occasions, but he refuses to change. She can't imagine leaving him, as she loves him immensely, but can't stand him when he is drunk. The question of what she should do is an internal trouble, and the answer is not always as simple as it seems.

Internal problems are not new. They have been there since the start. Let's examine an ancient example from Hinduism. Arjuna, a great and noble warrior, was chosen by Krishna (Hindu God) to fight a battle against evil, and the evil was his own siblings and relatives. It is the most complex example of internal trouble. Arjuna, both a great warrior and a good human being, is asked to take the lives of his cousins, uncles, teachers, grandsons, and more for the good of humanity. How can a good man harm his own family and friends? No throne is big enough for a righteous man to destroy his loved ones. But he must do it, or else evil will prevail. The citizens will suffer if he doesn't fight. To help Arjuna overcome his internal trouble, Krishna gives him wisdom, and that wisdom is called the Bhagavad Gita—the most holy scripture of Hindus.

However, we are not as great as Arjuna, nor do we have the same questions he once had. The wisdom shared with him is excellent, but it may or may not be relevant to us.

During most of our internal troubles, we lose our

rationality or our ability to think clearly. Why is that? Because we were never prepared for it. A man is never taught what to do or when he needs to choose between his wife and mother. A woman is never taught how to deal with an alcoholic husband whom she loves deeply. The problem comes to light one fine day, and we find ourselves struggling and confused.

So what do you do? How do you prepare yourself better? Please note that I am saying 'prepare'. A teacher can only *prepare* his or her students. A teacher does not always set the examination. It's the students' ability to answer the questions and the number of mistakes they make while answering them.

To be prepared for such troubles, one should develop a helpful nature. Be a good listener. Be sympathetic to others. You will find people around you who are going through such internal troubles. Be with them and observe what they are going through. Learn from their mistakes and offer them support. Do not think for one second that you're better than them or wonder why they are behaving this way. Developing this helpful nature is not for them; it is for you. You must look for people around you who are going through a tough time. People, who have lost someone dear to them, people who are struggling to sustain their marriage, or people who are dealing with an addicted family member. If you look, you will find that we are surrounded by such people. You must approach them with humility and empathy. There is nothing you can do for them, but they can do a lot for you. They can help you identify different internal problems. By observing them, you can learn how to deal with such problems if they ever arise.

Just as a fighter trains and strengthens his arms by hitting them against a hard surface intentionally and by enduring pain, you should also put yourself in a position to see, observe, and help those who are facing internal conflict, thereby being better prepared for them. One does not know what trouble will come their way, but they can only be prepared for it.

Now, this may not solve your trouble, but you will no longer be scared of it when it arises. Why? Because you know that problems exist, and you have simply not faced one yet. Understanding the problem is half the battle won. This is not just relevant to internal troubles, but also to external troubles. It makes your life much easier simply by understanding what sort of problem you are facing.

Let's go back to the first question: 'Whom do we go to when we need advice?'

Please take a moment to reconsider. When you understand your problems better, you solve them more effectively. At this stage, the question itself will become irrelevant.

No one can tell you what to do when you are facing trouble. Others can only tell you what you might be going through, and not what your real problem is. Why? Because they are not you and do not have the same life as you. Their circumstances may differ from yours. You might be an orphan, have had a rough childhood, lived in abject poverty, received no education, or have a learning disability. You must understand your own troubles and find a solution for them.

If you have an external problem, look for an external solution and don't waste your energy looking for an internal one. The same goes for internal problems. When you have an internal problem, don't try to solve it through external things.

THE SECOND STEP

Understanding the problem is only the first step. If you are suffering and looking for an answer, I am sure this would not be your first stop. I have personally listened to hundreds of different people, gurus, and enlightening podcasts. They all tell you how to find your problem and sometimes tell you what your problem is, and we all nod our heads, saying, 'Yes! That's right, this is my problem.'

However, after a day or two, we forget about what we heard and continue to suffer. To explain it further, let me give you an example: if you have a headache and visit a doctor, the doctor asks about the symptoms and tells you, 'Yes, it is a headache'. You relax your mind for a few seconds and think, 'Yes, he understands my problem', but then the doctor sends you home without medication.

If you look carefully, we are all visiting the same type of doctor who understands our problem. But does he really? We relax for a bit after consulting the doctor, and then he/she sends us away. The next morning, we have a headache again. Why? Because understanding is not enough, fixing it is imperative.

Understanding your problem is the first step; the second is understanding its effects and resolving them.

Just as we find a little peace within ourselves by knowing what our problem is, we can ease its effects by understanding them. This works for both internal and external problems. However, we will only focus on internal problems here. Some of the most common effects of an internal problem are sadness, anger and guilt. These feelings or effects are the most common, yet the most complex.

Sadness

When we discuss sadness, only two questions come to mind. First, why am I sad? Second, how can I not be sad?

To answer these questions, we have to understand what sadness is. Sadness is what makes us incomplete.

For example, a child gets sad and starts crying when his mother stops him from going outside to play with his friends. Think about why he really becomes sad. Does he become sad because his mother stopped him from doing something? No, he gets sad because he imagined himself playing with his friends, and now his imagination will not turn into reality, thus making him sad.

You might debate about the child's example. So, let's take a more realistic and relevant scenario. Imagine yourself as a kid: how did you imagine your future, and is your present exactly like how you imagined it? Or try to think about your future now: is it looking like what you wished for or imagined it to be? Keep thinking about it, and you will be full of sadness. Now, how can you be sad about something you only imagined? As kids, we all imagined having the best job when we grew up, the best car in the world, and the most beautiful, loving partner. The sadness starts to crawl in when you realise something is missing or is unfulfilled.

To understand this further, let's use death as our following example. Apart from a few exceptions, we all love our parents, don't we? Our father and mother. Have you reached that stage in your life where you have realised that one day your parents will no longer be with you, if not already? If you have not, then you must know that there will come a day when your parents will die.

Now, I suggest you think about the fact that one day our parents will die. When you continue to think about it, pay close attention to your thoughts. There will be some common thoughts, such as, 'I will be all alone'; 'who will I go to when I am sad?'; 'who will I call and tell all my problems to?'; 'who will tell me that they love me?'; and many more.

Did you realise something? Take a moment to think about it. Observe the thoughts that come to your mind.

Most of us will not think that our parents will miss us because they are dead. This feeling of death brings sadness, immense sadness. However, we don't get sad for the person who died, but for how it makes us feel incomplete.

Please understand that I am not trying to make you feel bad about yourself, but rather to explain what sadness is.

You may feel sadness if one of your parents passes away. You may realise that understanding sadness will not help your pain. It will not bring your loved one back. The sadness is permanent. There is nothing you can do to fill that missing piece because that person will never return. Before you succumb to these thoughts, pause and recall what we discussed earlier. The sadness does not arise from the person who died. It originates from within, from the feeling of incompleteness. Think about this statement again: 'I miss you'. The sadness is coming from the 'I' and not from their absence. You don't feel sad because your parents will miss you; you feel sad because you will miss them. You must ask this question: whose loss is greater: theirs or yours? And who is truly feeling sad at this moment? Them or you? The sadness stems from the sense of incompleteness that follows when someone you love is no longer there.

Now, if you are currently feeling sad, take a moment to ask yourself what is causing it. Or just remember to ask yourself the next time: 'Why am I feeling sad?' Similar to every problem in the world, knowledge and understanding make it better. Merely knowing is not enough; understanding is essential as well. Knowing I am sad about this or that is not enough; why am I sad is more important.

Why are we afraid of the dark? Because we don't know what will come out of it. Knowing and understanding make us feel better.

Do you know why married people should have children? I request that you reconsider it in the context of what I said before. Not only because we have a sexual desire, but also because we are biologically made to reproduce, that is there; however, if we look deeply, it has a bigger psychological impact on us.

You must have heard this saying many times: 'We gave or would give to our child what we never had.' You must have. And why is that? Is it because the child asked for it? And as parents, it is our duty to provide them with what they ask for? No, in most cases, the child doesn't even know about the existence of that desire or wish. Only the parents know, and they give it to their child because they are fulfilling what they missed in their own lives. We tend to provide what makes us sad. So, we provide our child with everything that fills that emptiness within us, justifying it in the name of the child.

I have no intention of suggesting that what parents do is wrong. I am simply stating a fact. This process of fulfilling our sense of incompleteness by providing for others is what we call coping with sadness indirectly. Another reason we have children is to cope with sadness directly. You must have heard people say, 'Who will continue our legacy?' or 'Who will carry on our family name?'

When we consider these statements, one thing comes to mind: we believe we are doing something noble, something right. We cannot allow our heritage and wealth to go to waste. Isn't it right? What could be wrong with leaving your child your name and your money? There is nothing wrong with it, as long as it doesn't come with expectations or personal needs attached.

But does it? If you are a child or a parent, I encourage you to ask yourself these questions. As a parent, if you decide to give your assets to your child, do you do so because it's yours and you want it to grow? Or do you want them to enjoy it? If you are a child, ask yourself, why have I received everything I have?' Are there any expectations attached to it? Or is it an act of pure love from my parents?

Now, as parents, it would be hard to realise it. Because our parents told us that whatever they did was for our betterment. So, as parents, we simply do what we are told without questioning it. We buy our child an expensive car, not because they need it. But it makes us happy to do that for our child. The child has no involvement in it.

To better understand, I recommend that everyone visit an

elderly care facility. You will find two types of old-age people there—first, the happy kind; and second, the sad and grumpy kind. The difference between them is not because one is sick and old, while the other is not. They are all sick and old, but why is one happy and the other not? Before I answer this, I'd like to point out that both types would be happy to live with their children and grandchildren. Both types will like more family visits. However, the primary difference between the happy and the sad is that the former expects something in return for what they have done throughout their lives, while the latter doesn't. The sadness stems from not being able to live the life they had imagined. The non-realisation of their imagination into reality causes sadness—the imagination that was fuelled by expectations from people and life in general.

Let's take a moment to process this all.

Expectation is not a bad thing, but one must choose carefully, as it often brings sadness along.

Before we get distracted further, let me circle back to the point under discussion. We have children to enhance our happiness and reduce the sadness within ourselves. Now it's not a bad thing to have children, because it helps reduce the sadness within us. But we must do that knowingly; otherwise, it will just bring more sadness.

As I mentioned above, knowing the symptoms is not enough; understanding them is essential as well. Knowing that you are sad is beneficial, but understanding the reason behind your sadness is equally crucial.

Here is the tricky part. I know I am sad; I know why I am sad. But how do I not be sad? There is one more important thing we must understand before we discuss how to remove sadness. People often speak of sadness and happiness in conjunction, when in reality they are very different. Entirely different actions cause each. Do not make the mistake of thinking that if you are not sad, you will be happy.

You can be sad or not, but happiness has nothing to do with it. It is a different matter altogether. You will often hear people say that when you are sad, you should do what makes you happy and have some fun. We have all listened to and tried this advice, but how many of us can say for sure that it has permanently alleviated our sadness? It is like being hungry, and someone offers you two glasses of water. It will fill your stomach, and you might not feel hungry for some time, but after a while, you will feel hungry again. Now, this doesn't mean water is not essential; however, you need food to satisfy your hunger, not just water. You need water when you are thirsty. Similarly, please don't get confused between sadness and happiness.

I would reinstate this again, not being sad does not mean being happy.

So, how can we not be sad?

I want you to think carefully and hard about the examples above. You will realise that sadness always appears to come from outside you and move inward. But that is not the case. Sadness originates from within and manifests outward. That's the tricky thing about it, and that is why it is so hard to get rid of it. Have you heard the saying, 'You can only give what you have?' Sadness is the prime example of that. Sadness comes from within and surrounds our body like an aura.

Understanding that sadness originates from within is, in itself, a significant relief. How? Because the only thing you can change is yourself and what's within. As human beings, we only possess the capability to change ourselves and what's within us, not others or what's outside. We can only change how we feel inside and not how others feel inside. We can only control our actions and not those of others.

If sadness originates from within us and the only aspect we can truly change is ourselves, it follows that we have the ability to lessen the sadness we feel. By identifying and understanding the source of our sadness, we can work towards resolving it. However, this leads us to an important question: how do we achieve this?

The answer is through practice–yes, you read it right–by practising to change what is within you and what is creating sadness. Things like expectations don't disappear overnight. If I or someone else tells you to stop expecting from today, it would mean nothing, and you will continue to expect things from others or from life itself. You have to practice, not to expect every day. The unfulfillment will not go away in a day or two. It may take weeks, years or sometimes a lifetime to go away.

I am not sure about many things in the world, but I am sure that the things that are said the easiest are the hardest to do, and practising is one of them.

Practice is something we have all heard about throughout our lives. Phrases like 'practice makes perfect', 'the more you practice, the better you get', 'practice before exams', and 'practice before matches' are considered in high regard, even in a sexual context. So why do we need reminders to practice in every aspect of our lives? Is it because we are so forgetful that we need constant nudges to remember that practice improves our skills? Not quite. We are reminded of this because practice is challenging. These reminders help ensure we don't become weary of the process and give up, whether consciously or unconsciously.

The only thing we can change and control is ourselves. Then, by consciously practising over time to remove the elements of sadness within us, we can reduce it to a minimum.

Another critical thing to remember is that we are not perfect; we all have our flaws. The world around us is not ideal either. And no matter what we do, our circumstances will keep giving birth to new elements of sadness within us. Therefore, practising changing what's within us is a lifelong process. Do not think we have removed a component of sadness within us, and a new one will not arise. It does not matter how much we have changed ourselves; sadness will continue to engulf us, and we must adapt accordingly.

Now, before we get caught up in negativity and start to lose hope, let's consider an example. Can you ever stop feeling the need to eat? Can you eliminate the hunger your body feels? How many meals have you had since you were born? I'd assume many, and yet, aren't you tired of eating?

Have you ever asked yourself, 'When will I stop feeling hungry?' No, right? You simply know that no matter how much you eat, you'll continue to feel hungry every day for the rest of your life.

Now, let's examine sadness and hunger through the same lens. How many times do we worry that we will feel hungry tomorrow and have to eat? Not many. Another question: how many of us think of feeling hungry and eating as a task? Not many. And why is that? Because we have realised that we will continue to feel hungry until we die, and for that reason, we have to eat throughout our lives. Realising and accepting this fact made it easy. Similarly, if we acknowledge that sadness is a part of our lives and continue to practice changing ourselves from within to remove that element of sadness, it will become easier. It will become an effortless task. Some people, both enlightened and not, have also referred to it as 'the way of living', 'the art of life', and many other terms.

We must remember that sadness is a permanent state, and so should be our efforts to alleviate it. The sadness only dies when we die. And if you are a believer in reincarnation and the next life, then sadness will continue to be there, too.

Lastly, remember, it is only you who can reduce your own sadness; no one else can. So, look inside and not outside. Discover and acknowledge the sadness within you. Recognise why you are feeling sad and what's causing it, and practice daily to eliminate that sadness.

Anger

It's one of the most common feelings and the most misunderstood one. As soon as we hear anger, we say 'bad'. We are taught and told by everyone from a young age that anger is destructive. We are told not to be angry. The person who gets angry is often perceived as a bad person and is seen as lacking the ability to control their emotions.

It's astonishing to see how people deal with anger. What is the best way to deal with a problem? Let's not discuss it and simply dismiss it by labelling it as bad. We must understand that the outcome of anger is wrong, but not anger in itself.

How many of us have heard this from someone we know 'This person has anger issues?' Let's think about it more carefully. Do parents never get angry with their children? Do the brother and sister not get angry with each other? Do the husband and wife not get angry with each other? Now, these are all beautiful relationships, and most people in them don't intend to cause harm to one another. In that sense, anger—when it comes from love and not ego—often serves the betterment of the other person.

So, does it make a mother a bad person for getting angry at her son for pushing another child off a slide? Would it be wrong for a wife to be furious if she caught her husband cheating?

My reason for providing such examples is to help you understand that, before we can understand anger, we must remove the taboo surrounding it. It is not as bad as you think. It is a natural emotion.

Please understand that I am not promoting anger or justifying it. It is essential to acknowledge it and understand it. If you search for anger around yourself in an aware state of mind, you'll realise two things: people who frequently express their anger often end up in jail, and those who never express it at all often end up in psychiatric hospitals.

The problem lies with our control over it, and how do you control something without understanding it!

Unlike sadness, anger comes from outside and does not reside within us permanently. It only emerges when needed and lasts for as long as required. Anything we experience beyond that is not anger. It could be violence, forced actions, or even simply frustration.

So what is anger?

Anger is nothing but a defence mechanism of any being. Sounds simple, doesn't it?

Let's try to understand it in detail. Any living being who gets angry is reacting to something being stolen or taken away from them, whether internally or externally. When I say 'any living being', I include all sources of life, including animals, humans, fish, birds, plants and more.

Before you jump to the conclusion that not all animals and plants get angry, you must know that not all living beings have the ability to express anger equally. However, every living being becomes angry when you try to steal or take something vital from them, whether it is an internal or external possession.

Now, before we get into other species, let's focus on humans. Why are we angry?

As mentioned earlier, anger is simply a defence mechanism to protect us. It is neither bad nor good. It is a natural reaction.

We must understand how stealing is related to anger. We must also distinguish anger from other emotions. Let's understand this with the help of an example. If someone slaps you, what will you feel? Angry? No, you will feel hurt, and because someone stole your right to protect yourself, you will get angry. Let me provide the same example with different characters. If a mother slaps her child for misbehaving, what will the child feel? Hurt or anger? Will he cry out in anger or hurt? Do you understand the difference between hurt and anger?

On this particular occasion only, I will give you a personal example: as a kid, I used to attend a school where beating kids was considered normal. Growing up, getting beaten up by teachers was considered normal for my friends and me. Not only that, we even treated it as an achievement. We used to count how many times we would get beaten up for something as small as forgetting a book. We didn't get angry at being slapped; in fact, we enjoyed it and framed it as an accomplishment.

I will not delve into the details of whether beating is bad or if we are unstable human beings. What I am trying to illustrate with this example is the distinction between hurt and anger. For us, being beaten was not something we were losing; it was something we were receiving. As such, we didn't get angry. The emotion we felt was hurt, not anger.

So what makes one angry, and what gets stolen?

If someone tries to take away what is internal to you—your self-respect, your peace, your ideology, your thoughts, or anything you hold dear within—you feel anger. Being robbed of your belongings can also make you angry. Examples of belongings include your body, your child, your money, your property, and anything you consider a personal possession.

It is essential to understand the differences between anger, disappointment, and frustration. As we often mistake one for the other.

Let's take some more examples to understand anger by knowing what it's not. When your partner forgets your birthday or anniversary, do you feel angry or disappointed? When you come back from work after a long, hard day and see your house is a mess or there are no groceries in the fridge, do you get angry or frustrated?

Another thing we commonly mistake anger for is violence. Anger is a reaction to an action. But violence is the action that causes reactions. I do not support violence, but I am a strong advocate of anger. Violence can cause anger, but anger cannot cause violence.

Now, why is it important to understand anger and distinguish it from other feelings? Because we must identify the problem before we can fix it.

So what is the right question? How do we not get angry at all? Or how do we manage our anger?

It is impossible to eliminate your defence mechanism. Even if one manages to do so, it is not a good idea, because we no longer live in a society of angels and enlightened beings.

If we read any religious texts and spiritual material, we will soon realise something: they all have one thing in common; they all talk about not giving in to our emotions. Do not react if something is done to you. Be separate from your emotions, detach yourself from attachments. If a man comes running towards you and tries to steal your watch, you must not give in to your emotions or get angry. One must live in the moment and should simply let it go. Even in modern times, we are being taught to let go. I have recently read a few books about letting go, and I assume you have too. They are very popular these days.

If we continue our search, we will also find that we must not live in the past or the future. What an idealistic view, such a noble practice. The first time I read, heard, or thought about it, I found it almost revolutionary. Many religious gurus and scholars have also said that nonviolence is the essence and that anger is the enemy of humankind, correct?

But we must ask some critical questions before unquestioningly accepting the practices preached by these noble scholars and religious advocates.

First, how effective are these practices in today's world? At the time these practices were created, life was different.

Second, are these practices only meant to be performed by men? If not, why have there been no examples of women given in these practices?

Lastly, those who preach such practices, have they achieved the stage of total detachment and complete non-violence?

It is crucial to understand the importance of detachment and not giving in to your emotions. But it is fundamentally flawed in today's society. These preaching's are nothing but a technique to manipulate the poor and sufferer.

Let me explain this bold statement with an example: an 18-year-old girl kidnapped from her hometown, sold to a city or country she has never been to, and on the verge of being forced into prostitution. Now, imagine a guru, a yogi, a scholar, a priest, or a monk telling the girl, 'This is all imaginary, pain is temporary, you should not give in to your emotions, live in the present moment, one should forgive to overcome,' and many more fine and glorious words of wisdom.

Now, do not make the mistake of thinking this is an imaginary situation; it is not an exception; it is not a one-of-a-kind thing. This happens a thousand times every day around the world. Children, girls and women every day around the globe get sold as part of human trafficking and are raped for months before they are killed or pushed into prostitution.

Now, the critical question as human beings is: should we teach these girls to be empathetic, patient, detached from their emotions, forgiving, and to not get angry? Or should we teach them how to fight for what is right? And how to channel their anger in the right direction?

If these gurus or priests are speaking the ultimate truth and have reached that stage of enlightenment, then they should also teach these girls and women about empathy and detachment from emotions, not just the men. The truth is, they cannot. Their preaching doesn't apply in this scenario or in the world we live in today.

The primary purpose of this is to understand that while information from the past may have been valuable, it does not necessarily apply to today's context. You may choose not to harm others, but the world may come to harm you. Questioning what is relevant today is as important as believing in something.

Now, let's think about the question from a fresh perspective: how do we not get angry at all? Or how do we manage our anger?

Before we delve into management, let's briefly clarify our current understanding of anger. It is not a seed that is resting in your subconscious and waiting to be watered. It is not a sign of evil, nor is it a result of bad karma. It is not something that will hinder our progress to reach enlightenment, and it is definitely not one of the greatest sins a human can commit. Anger is a reaction to something being taken away from us, it can be something internal or something that belongs to us.

Now that we know what it is not, let's focus on how to manage it. We manage anger by addressing its root cause: a sense of belonging.

Loss of belonging leads to the rise of anger as a defence mechanism. We must consider and prioritise our belongings carefully so that this defence mechanism only activates with intention.

What does 'consider your belongings' mean? It means we must be aware of what we acquire as our own. The more we acquire, the greater the risk of theft or damage. We cannot live without belongings, but we can certainly limit them. The amount of belongings depends on one's capacity to handle them. Some of us may have more than others.

When we talk about acquiring belongings in life, we must recognise that it is not just about buying more cars or larger parcels of land, but also the relationships we form along the way. We acquire different relationships at different stages of our lives. As children, we form relationships with our parents; later on, we form relationships with friends, partners, and kids. Calling them belongings may sound a little harsh, but do they not belong to you? Do we not take care of them? Do we not talk to them as if they are ours? And lastly, do we not get angry if something happens to them?

We don't always get the chance to choose our belongings, such as our parents and siblings. In most cases, they are considered good belongings, but in some cases, they are not. The other belongings we acquire are chosen, so we must be aware of what we are choosing.

Similar to considering our belongings, prioritising them is equally important. One must think carefully of what belongs to him or her, and if they were to let some belongings go, in what order would that be? Understanding what truly matters to us allows us to recognise what doesn't. When something is taken from us, it becomes clear whether it was of real importance. If it wasn't significant, we are less likely to feel anger about its loss. By reflecting on our priorities, we can reduce the likelihood of becoming angry.

Let me share an interesting story with you. Once upon

a time, two friends, let's call them A and B, would come to a park every evening to play with their friends. They enjoyed it very much. Their favourite game was racing each other, as they both loved to run. They both grew up, but their love for running never faded. Every evening, they would get together and run for hours. One day, A learned about an event called a marathon. He got excited and told B all about it. They both became thrilled and decided to participate. They agreed to take part in a 50 km marathon and began training and practising every day. They imagined themselves crossing the finish line countless times.

Finally, the day arrived. They were both super excited and well-prepared. The marathon began, and they started running. There they were, finally living the dream. A couple of hours into the marathon, they hit a rough patch. A, who had introduced the marathon to B, stepped on a stone. His ankle twisted, and he fell straight on his face. B rushed to him, helped him up, and saw his face bleeding. B wiped the blood away and asked, 'Are you alright?' Then he asked, 'Will you be able to run?' A said yes and resumed running. A few steps later, A fell again, since his ankle was broken. B said, 'Let me take you to the doctor,' but A refused. B insisted, but A asked B to continue running and finish the marathon. B, being the good friend that he was, wanted to stay with him, but A urged B to continue without him. After a few minutes of arguing, B realised that A was right and that he should continue running and finish the marathon.

B ran on, feeling sad. But as the finish line came into view, B became excited and happy. He was the first to finish the marathon. The crowd cheered and surrounded him. He hesitated for a moment but eventually celebrated. After some time, his happiness began to fade. He expected something more. But that feeling wasn't there. As he reflected, he realised that his dream was not to run a marathon or to come first. It was to run for hours alongside his best friend.

In our lives, there are times when we successfully complete the marathon and moments when we dream but ultimately fall short. We should not feel guilty for not finishing, nor should we be angry about being left behind.

Now, to end this, I would repeat this once again. Anger is not all bad; it is as natural as breathing. We should understand it and not get confused by what it's not. If we understand anger and its origins, we can manage it more effectively. If we prioritise our belongings, then we won't get angry at things that don't matter. And the best way to do this is on your own. Talk to yourself, observe yourself and manage yourself better.

Guilt

People on their deathbed have a lot of regrets, don't they? We have all heard them say things like: 'I wish I had spent more time with my family,' 'I wish I had done this for my partner,' 'I wish I had done what I wanted to do.'

If we pause for a moment and ask ourselves this question: what is the most important thing to a dying person? And does that align with the statements mentioned above?

Dying is inevitable. However, some choose to die with a smile on their face, while most of us pass on carrying guilt and regret within us. If dying is such a crucial event in our lives, then isn't it important to do it properly? To die with a smile, one must first let go of all regrets and guilt.

The only way to free ourselves from guilt is to sit quietly and reflect: 'What do I regret? Am I feeling guilty about something?' Speak to yourself and ask, 'Why am I feeling this way?' and 'What was the situation, and what did I wish had happened but did not?'

Once you have asked yourself these questions, you can do one of three things: first, justify your actions; second, learn from them and try not to repeat them; and third, let go.

Justify your actions: to let go of guilt, one might claim they had no choice or that they acted under extreme circumstances. They may regret what they did, but they had little to no control over the situation. In such cases, a person can release their guilt by recognising that their actions were a result of circumstance. For example, being forced to kill someone in self-defence and later feeling regret. One can say, 'I didn't want to do that, but I had no choice but to save myself; I have a family to look after.' In such a scenario, one let go of the guilt by justifying it.

Learn and don't repeat: the second way to let go of guilt is to accept it and choose not to repeat the action. It's rare, but it does happen. Let me share an example of someone I know. There was a woman who had a fairly religious upbringing, where drinking alcohol was considered wrong. Once she became an adult and independent, she decided to try it. After getting drunk three or four times, she began to feel deeply guilty about her actions and decided never to drink again, and she hasn't touched alcohol since.

In fact, many addicts who are now sober have gone through a similar experience. They regretted their actions, recognised their guilt, and that realisation became the turning point in their recovery. Please note, in this example,

I am not suggesting that alcohol is bad. It is entirely a matter of personal choice.

Letting go: just like guilt, letting go is also tricky. Letting go of guilt comes into play when neither acceptance nor blame helps. You might be wondering, "How does one let go of guilt?"

Think of a soldier in battle who kills his opponent without knowing whether that man was good or bad, or whether he had a family waiting at home. He does it to protect his country. Similarly, in some cases, guilt must simply be released, neither accepted nor denied.

Have you seen the film about the creation of the first atomic bomb? When guilt grows so immensely that it threatens your very own survival, you must let it go without reasoning. It becomes your foremost duty to protect yourself.

Although I do not usually quote religious scriptures, in this instance, it feels necessary. I'm not a follower of gurus, yogis, or spiritual teachers, but I hold deep respect for religious texts.

"Karmanyevaadhikaaraste Maa phaleshu kadaachana."

A statement derived from the *Bhagavad Gita*, it means *'You have the right to perform your duties (or actions), but not to the fruits of your actions.'*

To me, this means that there are moments in life when being right or wrong becomes irrelevant, and you simply have to do what is required. In the context of guilt, there are times when a person feels guilt and is honest enough not to blame others, yet too fragile to accept it. But you must survive; therefore, you must let it go.

So how do we do that? If you find yourself in such a situation, you might be waiting for me to give you a definitive solution.

Unfortunately, I cannot tell you, but fortunately, I know someone who can, and that's you.

I call guilt the magic emotion, as it is the trickiest of them all. Unlike anger and sadness, it doesn't have any visible or physical appearance. We don't often know about its existence, but only feel its worst effects.

Out of all the emotions, guilt is the hardest to understand and overcome. Why? Because unlike other emotions, we rarely show it, and, in most cases, we aren't even aware of its existence. So, what is this destructive magic? At its core, guilt is the result of our inability to satisfy ourselves. We have heard these phrases many times: 'He made me feel guilty for doing that' or 'I am feeling guilty for not doing this,' haven't we? Now, have you wondered what it means when we say the word 'guilty'? What exactly do we feel? Naming something is easy; understanding is not so.

Why do I call it tricky or complex? Although it arises within, it can be caused and triggered by both internal and external forces. It can be as simple as 'I am on a diet but ended up eating a lot of junk food, and now I feel guilty,' or as complicated as moving to another country to give your parents a better life, only for them to pass away with you being unable to attend their funeral.

Many wise men and women have spoken about anger, pain, sadness, pleasure, and desire, yet little has been said about guilt. I am not as wise as those religious scholars, motivational speakers, or gurus; perhaps that is why it holds such great importance to me.

Guilt is like a pothole on our journey, often invisible, yet large enough to damage the shock absorbers. When exploring guilt and its relevance in our lives, it is essential to recognise that regret and guilt are closely connected. Regret is an instant reaction to a situation, and guilt is its long-term effect on the self.

One typical example of this is when a husband shouts at his wife over a trivial issue. He instantly regrets his actions, and as a result, continues to feel guilty about what he did. The guilt might last for days or even his lifetime. I completely understand if some of the women don't agree with me on this.

I would be lying to you if I said, "Do this, and you will get rid of your guilt." All I can do is explain what guilt is and suggest what you might do with it. Only you can teach yourself how to do it, and no one else. I am not in your shoes; my feelings about things are not the same as yours. My circumstances are different from yours.

However, once you understand and realise what guilt is, you are fully equipped with the tools you need. Do not look for an external solution for an internal problem. Look internally, talk to yourself, and understand your guilt. Decide what you want to do with it and how you want to get rid of it.

It is important to remember that the only person who can truly help you is yourself, which is why I say, 'me for myself'. I am not against taking help. I have taken help myself. We all need support, but it should be to understand, not to rely on someone else to do what we must do ourselves.

One last story

To conclude the subject of problems, I would like to share a story. The story of Hiranyakashyap (a powerful demon) and Narasimha (an avatar of Krishna, the Hindu god). The story unfolds as follows: the demon was granted a boon that he could not be killed during the day or at night, not by a human or an animal, and not inside the house or outside. Thus, to kill that demon, Krishna took the form of Narasimha, a being that is half human and half lion, and killed him in the evening, a time that was neither fully day nor fully night and on the window frame, with half of his body inside the house and half outside.

Similarly, our problems are like the demon 'Hiranyakashyap'; they don't go away with spirituality or science alone. Not by consulting a psychiatrist or visiting a guru. Neither by complete indulgence nor by complete renunciation of our society. You must take on the form of 'Narasimha' and find a balance between science and spirituality to solve your problems. You can only solve your problems if you take time to understand, learn about, and accept them. You cannot get better by simply ignoring them or by blindly believing something. You must find a balance, both within and outside. In today's world, we passionately debate whether the glass is half full or half empty; however, we often overlook the water itself. The balance lies in seeing the water, understanding it, and drinking it, not in proving our perspective to others.

KEY TAKEAWAYS

1. Two types of problems: Internal vs. External
   - Internal problems are inner conflicts: dilemmas, emotional struggles, and ethical questions that can only be solved internally. They are complex because they involve one's beliefs, identity, and values.
   - External problems are practical, outward issues, such as unpaid taxes, job loss, or expenses, which can usually be resolved by concrete action or help from others.
   - Mistaking one for the other wastes energy; external problems require external solutions, while internal ones necessitate internal solutions.

2. Why internal problems hurt more
   - Internal troubles (e.g., choosing between wife and mother, or loving an alcoholic husband) feel harder because they pit two cherished values against each other.
   - We're rarely taught how to handle them, so we're unprepared when they arise.

3. Understanding is preparation
   - Observing others' inner conflicts, listening, and helping sympathetically is like 'training' for your own internal battles.
   - Seeing how others handle pain offers lessons without arrogance ('It's not for them, it's for you').
   - Knowing a problem exists doesn't solve it, but it makes you less afraid and more prepared to face it.

4. Sadness as incompleteness
   - Sadness arises not from what happens but from the gap between imagination/expectation and reality; a sense of incompleteness.
   - This applies to small things (such as a mother stopping her child from playing) and big things (like the loss of a parent).
   - Accepting that sadness originates within, rather than from external events, is the first step toward reducing it.

5. Practice, not quick fixes
   - Like hunger, sadness is recurring and lifelong; you don't 'cure' it once and for all.
   - Continuous practice, self-awareness, and adjusting your inner responses gradually reduce sadness.
   - Accepting sadness as a lifelong process makes it feel less like a burden and more like a natural rhythm of life.

6. Anger as a defence mechanism
   - Anger itself is neutral and natural; its outcomes may be harmful, but the feeling is not inherently 'bad'.
   - It arises when something you consider 'yours' (inner values or outer belongings) feels stolen or violated.

- Understanding the difference between anger, hurt, disappointment, frustration, and violence helps you manage them rather than suppress them.
- Reducing anger involves consciously limiting and prioritising your 'belongings', including relationships, to lower your vulnerability to loss.

7. Guilt as the 'Invisible' Emotion
   - Guilt is more complicated to detect than sadness or anger because it leaves no clear outward trace, yet can deeply corrode your well-being.
   - It is a long-term effect of regret; the internal outcome of being unable to satisfy your own standards.
   - Three main ways to handle guilt:
     1. Justify (I had no choice),
     2. Learn and change (accept and don't repeat),
     3. Slash (let it go when it's too heavy to bear, as an act of survival).
   - Ultimately, only you can decide which approach works for your specific guilt.

8. Limits of traditional advice
   - Many spiritual or religious teachings (detachment, non-violence) were created in very different contexts and may not entirely align with today's harsh realities.
   - Questioning old practices and adapting them is necessary, especially when they're used to pacify the vulnerable instead of empowering them.

9. The "Narasimha" approach to problems
    - Neither pure spirituality nor pure pragmatism alone can solve life's problems.
    - Like Narasimha's hybrid form, you must combine internal understanding with external action to handle your troubles.
    - You must rely on balance, self-knowledge, and conscious choice, not blind tradition or blind activism.

10. The core message
    - Understand whether a problem is internal or external.
    - Prepare by observing others and practising inner change.
    - Act by applying the right kind of solution (internal work for internal problems; external action for external ones).
    - Accept sadness, anger, and guilt as natural emotions that are manageable through self-awareness and practice.
    - Ultimately, 'me for myself'. No one can resolve your inner conflicts for you, but you can equip yourself to handle them.

PART 2:
THE WHY & WHAT

'Why' and 'what' are two of the most common and simplest words used in the English language. However, when used in specific sentences, they pose some of the most challenging questions for humanity. Questions such as, 'What is God?' 'Why are we here?' and 'What is the purpose of our life?' Such questions have boggled humans for centuries. Many religious teachers, scholars, and philosophers have spent their entire lives pondering these questions and teaching us through their intellect and religious texts.

Another thing to consider is how satisfied we are with the answers we've received. Do we blindly believe what we are told, or do we dismiss it solely on the basis of our intellect? We must ask ourselves: Is there any credibility in religious scriptures, or are these scriptures and holy texts merely stories meant to prevent us from doing wrong? If that were the case, how could it be so? How could someone write a story so detailed and so deeply infused with wisdom? How could one do so unless the scriptures were the word of God?

Coming back to why and what, the two most important words of humankind. Science has taught us the importance of these words. To learn, the mind must ask questions. What is out there, and why is it out there? What is this, and why is that? Every time we discover something new, we see it and ask, 'What is this?' and then, 'Why is it?' For example, when humans first saw an aurora, they must have asked, 'What is this?' and then wondered why it occurs. In science, 'what' comes first and 'why' comes later.

To me, the *why* comes before the *what*. To go inward, which is to reach within ourselves, we must ask the *why* before we ask the *what*. The reason for this is that we are not trained to look inward. Throughout our lives, we are taught to look outward, meaning we reach for what exists beyond our bodies and toward the world around us. Therefore, most of us lack the ability to go inward. Techniques such as meditation were introduced to increase our awareness and our ability to go inward. However, these techniques are incomplete without the determination to understand, and that determination comes from the *why*.

Let us understand this with an example. Most of us, while scrolling on our phones, end up looking at some form of paid advertisement. The advertisement could be about joining a gym, downloading a new photo-editing app, or buying the latest gadget. Many of us have purchased such a product or service at least once, believing it to be useful or necessary. However, I feel confident in saying that more than 80 percent of us do not use that service for more than a week.

In this example, the *why* is the advertisement, and *what* is our action of purchasing the product or service. The reason we stopped using that product or service is that the *why* wasn't strong enough. The need to buy did not come from within but from an external influence. We did not download the app because we were actively looking for such a solution; rather, we downloaded it because the advertisement made us feel as though we were missing out.

Similarly, when we join a gym after watching a motivational video or advertisement, we often stop going after a week or two because our *why* is not strong enough. Therefore, before making any decision, we must ask ourselves: *Why do I want to do this?* Is it because I am influenced by someone else, or because I truly need it? Thus, identifying the reason behind our *why* is essential before proceeding.

Similarly, before asking more important questions about life, such as what God is, we should first ask, "Why do we want to know God?" Do I want to know what God is so that I can sound superior to others, or does the question of existence trouble me every day? Likewise, before asking what I am, we should ask why we want to know ourselves. Do I want to know myself because I saw a TED Talk that said, "You must find yourself," or is there something deeper troubling me that can only be resolved by knowing myself? Therefore, if you find a strong enough "why", you will be able to move in the direction of the "what". Otherwise, the effort will be temporary and the energy wasted.

A HUMBLE REQUEST

As this is a subject of great controversy and misconception, I request everyone, myself included, to be humble. To question and learn, we must humble ourselves. If you are coming from a rigid point of view or are simply here to strengthen your confirmation bias, reading further would be a waste of your time and energy, something we all lack these days. Therefore, I request that you read with curiosity and a learning mindset, rather than any other motive.

One must ask, what do you mean by being humble?

To understand humbleness in the context of philosophy, I would quote the words of a great teacher, Vikas Divyakirti: "The only thing we know for certain is that we don't know anything for certain, and we know that we don't know everything."

These words help us open ourselves to new ideas and give us the ability to learn more than we know. Therefore, I would like to repeat these words to myself and suggest that you read them aloud as well.

"The only thing I know for certain is that I don't know anything for certain, and I know that I don't know everything."

A great many scholars, religious teachers, gurus, and philosophers claim that what they say is the truth, and the only truth. I make no such claims.

WHO AM I?

The "I" here refers to what some call "Soul", some call "Ego", and some call "Ether". I call it "Energy"—something that is within us, which we cannot see and is not present in a tangible form.

As discussed earlier, to find "what", we must first ask "why". The 'why' differs from one person to another. My "why" might not be the same as yours. Why do you want to know yourself? This question can only be answered by you. Unlike others, I can't tell you why you should find yourself. Because if I do, I will be doing guesswork or simply lying. The reason to know must come from within, not from outside. If it comes from external sources, it is merely an influence, and influence doesn't last for long.

However, I can share my understanding of it with you and hope it will help you find yours.

As said by Robert A. Johnson, *gold can only be found in the dark*. The darkness here refers to anger, frustration, desire, disappointment and more. And within that darkness, one can find gold, which is willingness. The willingness to know and/or the willingness to change. To find the why, you must acknowledge your darkness, accept it, and tend to it. Ignoring it or simply dismissing it is the worst thing one can do.

Like visiting a doctor only when ill, individuals often discover their true selves in moments of confusion, pain, suffering, or simple curiosity. I can give you the ultimate book of happiness, but if you are already content with your life, you wouldn't even look at it. One eats when they are hungry, one sleeps when they are sleepy, and one finds oneself when they are …?

Let me walk you through a journey of someone I know. This gentleman started his journey as an atheist, which was shortly followed by knocking on every religion's doorstep. From not believing to becoming a complete devotee of God. From thinking that there is no God and that he controls his own destiny to believing that he is simply doing the will of God. From believing there is no such thing as a soul to believing that God resides within him in the form of a soul.

He shared that, for years, he had been swinging from one side to the other. From atheism to believing in Buddhism, Hinduism, Jainism and Christianity, yet peace was found in none. After every few years, he was in significant doubt, thinking, 'What if all this is wrong?' He was afraid: what if he died believing in the wrong thing? What if there is no Hell or Heaven? What if there is no God? Questions such as, 'If there is a God, then why are some kids born with a silver spoon and some born in poverty with disabilities?' created doubt. To justify this, he started to believe in past karma. No matter what he believed in, after a point, doubts arose. This was his darkness. Confusion, doubt and frustration. Within which he found his gold, and so can you in yours. The great doubt brought great revelation—the fear within led to peace.

Once we are determined to find out about ourselves, the journey becomes easier. The energy doesn't diminish.

The question remains, who are we, or who am I?

We are nothing but an amalgamation of the world around us. This may sound simple, but it is certainly not that straightforward.

So what does 'amalgamation of the world around us' mean? It means that we are composed of everything present around us: elements, people, knowledge, scenery, animals, light, and darkness. There is nothing original about us; we are a byproduct of the world and everything in it. Our thoughts originate from our experiences, our beliefs stem from our society, and our purposes arise from our insecurities. Before rejecting this idea, we must look at ourselves more carefully and ask these questions about ourselves:

How am I able to speak, read, write, and understand the language I use? Was it taught to me, or was I born with it?

Why do I follow my religion? Did I choose it while looking for God or because my parents followed it?

Can I survive without consuming what is in the world?

Have I ever created anything without using what the earth has to offer? Did I make iron, wood or trees, or am I simply consuming and modifying them?

Are my thoughts my own, or do they belong to my society and culture?

Am I knowledgeable because I was born with intelligence, or because my parents could afford to send me to school and college?

If we think sincerely and honestly, we will realise there is nothing inside our body that is not made up of what's outside it. The water, earth, fire, air, the people around us, their knowledge, and even the animals. It is because there are animals that we are called humans; otherwise, we might have called ourselves animals too.

Our entire existence is rooted in what surrounds us. Countless elements, seen and unseen, contribute to our being. Without our surroundings and all that they offer, we would never have come into existence. Imagine if Adam had lacked fresh water or fruit. Would he have survived long enough to bring forth life and, in doing so, pave the way for us?

However, the statement that we are nothing more than an amalgamation of the world around us appears to contradict certain prominent ideas, such as the belief that we are who we are because of our soul, which makes us unique. If we are merely the by-product of our surroundings, then why are two people who share the same surroundings still different? For example, two children born of the same parents should be identical, since their surroundings are essentially the same.

To understand why each one of us is unique while still being an amalgamation of the world around us, I invite you to imagine something: imagine yourself in a kitchen that has over 100 different types of vegetables, 50 types of spices, 25 types of oils, 15 types of meat, 10 types of utensils, and five types of knives. And you are asked to make soup. Now we all know what soup tastes like, correct? And you end up making delicious soup. The final result of the cooking process is the soup known as "Me", with a taste referred to as "I" or energy. After you, another person enters the same kitchen to recreate the same soup. Would that soup taste exactly like yours? Even if you give that person the exact recipe, one thing is certain: the two soups will not taste the same. Why is that? The same kitchen, the same ingredients, the same dish, and the same utensils could not produce the same dish.

The key difference between one individual and another lies in their circumstances, and for every person, those circumstances can be vastly different. One might be born near towering mountains, while another is born near the vast expanse of the ocean. One could come into a wealthy family with abundant resources, while another might be born into poverty, facing constant struggle. One might enjoy perfect health from birth, while another could face physical or mental challenges.

From a distance, looking at the Earth as a whole, it is the same for everyone. Yet the specific place and conditions into which you are born profoundly shape your experiences, opportunities, and challenges. These circumstances influence the "ingredients" you consume in life—both literally, like food and environment, and metaphorically, like knowledge, culture, and energy from the people around you. Some individuals may have access to abundance in one area but scarcity in another, while others face the opposite. Over time, these factors shape not only what you become but also how you perceive and interact with the world.

This does not mean that spirituality is unrelated to our lives. In fact, spirituality and religion guide us in choosing the best ingredients, as one wrong ingredient can impact the overall flavour. While the dish would still be recognised as a soup, its taste may not be as enjoyable.

This might be the weirdest example you have heard so far, but it was the simplest one I've encountered. If you can understand even some of what I am saying, then we are on the right track.

The key to knowing oneself is not through science nor religion alone. It lies between both of them. The term we use to define oneself is not important. We can call it whatever we desire. Debating what to name a waterfall while ignoring its beauty is a pure waste of time and energy.

To sum it up, we are an amalgamation of everything around us, and depending on our individual circumstances, we absorb it. This leads to our uniqueness. This uniqueness is a manifestation of the ingredients we consume. And all the ingredients have energy within them. At the same time, religion helps us distinguish between the good energy and the bad energy that ingredients contain.

Understanding the relationship between ingredients and energy is crucial, as is the role of religion in this context.

Therefore, to understand oneself, it is essential to grasp the concept of energy.

Energy

Everything around us carries some sort of energy: people, land, food, oceans, and mountains – everything carries some kind of energy.

Let's look at some ways we consume energy.

Through observation

Why do people feel relaxed when they see beautiful scenery? Why do so many go to the beach to unwind on a Sunday morning? Have you ever heard someone say they feel a sense of peace when visiting a church or temple? What we observe gives us energy. On the other hand, why do we feel sadness when we see images of famine or natural disasters? Why does witnessing someone mistreating their staff provoke outrage? Everything we observe and consume carries its own energy.

Through association

Numerous books have been written about this. And it's probably one thing each of us has heard from our parents as kids: "Don't hang out with bad people; make good friends that can influence your life positively." People carry energy; if you spend time with selfish people, you tend to absorb their energy. If you spend enough time with religious people, you will start becoming religious. Good or bad, you consume energy through association more than you think. If your best friend's partner cheats on them and your best friend is heartbroken, you may also feel enraged. This happens because you absorb their energy.

Through possession

The things we keep around us transfer their energy to us. One of the most common examples of this is our home garden. People feel relaxed and happy when they plant new things in their garden, take care of their plants, or even simply observe them. Why do you think people bring flowers to someone who is sick or is in the hospital? Flowers are not medicine; we cannot cure anyone by placing flowers near them, yet we still do. Why? Because they have good energy within them, and we absorb it.

Through eating

It's a famous saying, "You become what you eat." This means that everything you eat, drink, or inhale contains some form of energy. When we eat fresh fruit, we feel refreshed, and when we drink tea, we feel attentive. When we inhale the scent of burning incense, we feel relaxed. On the contrary, if we eat highly processed food, we feel stuffed and low on energy. Similarly, if we consume copious amounts of alcohol, we lose our senses.

Knowing that everything around us contains energy and we are made up of energy doesn't make religion or God irrelevant. On the contrary, it makes it even more relevant.

You may ask, 'How?' Because without religion, most of us will never know what energy should be consumed and what shouldn't. Have you ever realised that every region has its own religion? Why is that? Simply because, based on the regions' availability of resources, the religion suggested what one should do and what one shouldn't do. Isn't that the most significant difference in all religions? Lifestyle choices vary from one religion to another, depending on the region.

You cannot simply disregard the importance of religion and base everything on science. In fact, all the religious texts contain crucial information specific to their respective regions. For example, following Islam in extremely cold regions may pose practical challenges, while its practices align more comfortably with warmer climates. Similarly, for followers of Christianity, living in hot, arid environments can be demanding, as alcohol consumption in such conditions may lead to dehydration rather than provide warmth. If you see it from a broader perspective, it does make sense. If we simply do things or at least understand the things we do and why we do them, it can significantly benefit humanity. Have you seen the news lately? What do you think is really happening? It is not happening because of any religious dictate but because of our understanding of it.

Religion and sacred texts help us distinguish between the positive and negative energy contained in the things around us, depending on the region.

To understand who we are, we must incorporate both science and religion. The combination of nature and the spirit leads to the revelation.

Have you ever looked at a monk and thought, 'How can he be so calm and composed?' Now you probably know why. Because he is highly selective about what he consumes, observes, and associates with.

Thich Nhat Hanh, a renowned monk and peace activist, has beautifully and insightfully described the workings of the inner being. He said that we have various seeds of energy within us, and we must water them carefully and with awareness. If we water the right seed, it will grow, and the bad seed will remain dormant. The good seeds include peace, joy, empathy, love and more. The bad seeds are anger, sadness, despair, desire and more. It is up to us what we water and grow within.

Some may call it the seed, others the ego; I like to call it an amalgamation of energy that transforms into thoughts.

To become aware of the seeds within us, we employ various techniques, one of which is meditation.

Meditation

A technique to understand what's within. It's a popular exercise, known by many and understood by few. As mentioned above, there is energy within, and this energy manifests as thoughts, which in turn lead to actions. Meditation helps us understand our energy and the thoughts it generates. Thus providing us a better understanding of ourselves. Just as physical exercise helps us build our outer body muscles, meditation helps us build our inner body muscles. There are hundreds, if not thousands, of books written about meditation. I believe it has been overcomplicated and has become a commodity to be sold. One might not pay much for a simple exercise, so how about we make it complicated to increase its value? I am not saying that meditation is the easiest thing one can do, but it is definitely not as complex as it seems.

There are two essential things we must understand before we start learning about meditation, and before we practise it. First, it only helps us identify what's within and not change it. Second, one doesn't reach a higher state or enlightenment by meditating for long periods.

I can't emphasise enough that meditation helps us to simply identify and understand our energies. It does not change or transform it. Utilising and transforming the energy is a separate topic that we will discuss moving forward. Now that we know what meditation is *not*, we can focus on what it is.

Meditation is a two-step process:
First, isolation from the outside.
Second, focus on the inside.

Step 1: Isolation from the outside

Our bodies are continuously absorbing energy from the outside. In today's world, most energy consumption is involuntary. What that means is that we are not aware of what we are consuming. We often hear statements like, "I have a toxic work environment" or "toxic people surround me." This means that simply being near certain individuals allows their energy to seep into us, even without direct interaction. Imagine walking into a room where a team has just had a heated argument. The air feels heavy, conversations are clipped, and even if everyone is trying to act normal, you can sense the tension hanging in the space. That invisible weight of negativity can affect your mood, thoughts, and energy, showing just how much our surroundings influence us.

This is not limited only to people, but to everything. A lush green valley will exude positive energy, unlike a slum where poverty and suffering prevail.

Buddhism realised this long ago and introduced the concept of awareness. Which, in short, is to be aware of yourself so that you consciously consume energy. A monk's lifestyle is designed to support and increase this conscious consumption of energy. They focus on every action that they perform in their life, whether it is eating, sleeping, walking, watching or thinking.

Meditation is the name we give to our efforts to block all external energy consumption, regardless of its type.

Meditation technique

Many techniques have been developed over time. Some

may work better for one person, while others may not. I recommend the holding-of-breath technique. The method proceeds as follows: sit or lie down in a comfortable position and begin by breathing normally. Do not force yourself to take long or short breaths. Simply breathe as you usually do. After a few minutes, start holding your breath for a second or two as you breathe in (hold), breathe out (hold). Once you can do that, we shall move to the last step. Remember, the key is to do it as naturally as you can. Only breathe in as much as you usually do and only hold your breath for a second. The same goes for breathing out: do not try to exhale all the air. Exhale only the amount of air you usually do and hold your breath for a second or two.

Once you can do that comfortably, start counting from 1 to 10 and then reverse the count. Do this as you're breathing. You might notice two things: first, you may forget the count in the middle of your breathing. If that happens, start again. Second, you will get lost in your thoughts, but something interesting will also occur: when thoughts appear, you will forget to breathe. If that happens, your mind will break the thought and remind you to breathe. Once you realise that, start the breathing technique again. This technique will make you focus on yourself and stop the consumption of energy from outside.

If you continue the breathing technique for some time, you might realise that you have forgotten to count, you are not holding your breath, and you are simply breathing. That's when you will go inside, and all the energy within will start to appear.

Step 2: Focus on the inside

Once you successfully block all external energy, your focus shifts inward. You start to realise what is going on within yourself. You begin to feel things that you didn't even know existed. Just so you don't get confused, what you feel initially when you realise what's inside you, don't mistake it for something else, as it is just energy you have consumed. When we observe and focus on that energy, it may evoke different emotions and feelings. It is like going through your high school notebook, when you read your handwriting and the things you made note of, you imagine the classroom where you made them. Sometimes going through old things can be emotional, whether it's seeing an old notebook or old family pictures. Going inside and observing is precisely like that. Once you are aware of the bundles of energy within you, you can make informed decisions on how to release them.

Have you ever realised that when you try to meditate, you start to have weird thoughts? Things those are totally irrelevant to reality. The more you try to focus on not thinking, the more thoughts come into your mind.

Most of us think that we are unable to focus or meditate, and as a result, we give up. On the contrary, we are doing the correct thing. Meditation is a process of finding oneself, but when we look within, we often get confused and give up. All that is within us is energy that transforms into thoughts.

Meditation technique

After you have entered your body, begin by simply observing the energy. Avoid trying to control anything. The thoughts presented to you are reflections of what exists within. Or one can say it is your subconscious mind. Simply observe; not controlling is the key here. Not all thoughts will be positive, nor will all thoughts be relevant. But that is the reality of your inside.

Initially, the thoughts may not make sense, but if you continue to practice, you will begin to observe them from a third-person perspective and see what has been resting inside you for a long time.

If the thoughts are disturbing and are hindering your focus, then imagine yourself as an outline. An outline of your body sitting in the galaxy. Through this practice, you will be able to see your energy in a different form—in the form of colour and light. Simply notice them. Do not attempt to control or alter the energy, as this will disrupt your state of meditation.

The meditation technique will help you gain a deeper understanding of yourself. What does your inner self look like? What is it like to be self-aware? To know what is happening inside?

This is just one of the many techniques to help you become more aware of your inner thoughts and feelings. One last thing to remember is that there is no one-size-fits-all approach. You should experiment and discover what works best for you. It is crucial not to force yourself; true self-awareness develops naturally with patience, time, and consistent practice.

Half-battle won

To realise what's inside is half the battle won, and what to do with it is the remaining half.

There are two things you can do: either be very mindful of the energies you consume, or consciously release negative energy while actively cultivating positive energy. Conscious consumption involves adopting a restricted lifestyle, similar to that of a monk or a priest, in which they absorb only positive energy and feel at peace with it.

However, this presents a challenge for most of us. We are advised to live like monks while being surrounded by all kinds of energies. Monks and priests are not working nine-to-five jobs to provide for their families, taking their parents to the hospital, or worrying about taxes. They have created an environment where they only consume positive energy. If they were asked to live your life, they would also lose their peace, just as you do. This is why we need a solution for people like us, who have limited control over our surroundings and the energies we absorb. The solution is to regularly release negative energy so it doesn't accumulate, while continuing to seek and consume positive energy.

The five-element technique

The five-element technique is a method for harnessing positive energy without altering our surroundings. Through this technique, we can consume positive energies like a monk without having to live like one.

The basic concept behind this technique is to bring things closer to you without having to go to them. If you can't live near the mountains, then get the mountains near you. If you can't live near the ocean, bring the sea near you. This might not sound practical, as you cannot possibly move the mountains or the oceans; however, you can definitely get their energies closer to you.

To understand this further, let's explore the elements first. The five elements are air, water, fire, earth and space. Each element contains energy vital to our survival.

Our body and everything around us are made up of these elements. The mountain, the ocean, the land we stand on, everything. If we are close to a mountain, we can absorb its energy directly. However, even though we are physically far away from it, we can still harness similar energy as the mountain is composed of the same elements.

To practise this technique, we take these elements and use our imagination to absorb the energy of what is far.

Let's examine the elements one by one and learn to absorb their energy.

Earth Element: Take a bowl filled with soil and sit in a comfortable position. Close your eyes and place your hand in the bowl. As you feel the mud against your skin, imagine where it has come from. It could be part of a mountain, a grassy field, or even a desert. Visualise yourself touching the mountain, the desert, or the land where the grass grows while simultaneously feeling the soil in your hand.

With continued practice, you will begin to notice energy flowing from the bowl of soil into your hand. You may even feel as if you are truly touching the mountain or the land you are imagining. It is important to try this yourself before accepting or dismissing the effectiveness of this technique.

Water element: Similar to the earth element, fill a bowl

with water and follow the steps. Sit in a calm position, with no distractions. Put your palm into the bowl. Feel the water touching your skin. Relax your mind and imagine yourself sitting by a lake with clear, cold water flowing. Do not force yourself and continue breathing normally. Feel yourself touching the river or a lake. Imagine the energy from the water flowing to your hand, then throughout your entire body. With practice, you will be able to feel more and more energy flowing from the water to you. It is similar to seeing a mother's face while she holds her baby in her arms. You feel a sense of peace simply by looking. Every drop of water carries the same energy as the ocean. We just need to realise it.

Fire element: With the fire element, you can create a fire inside the bowl, but it may be risky. Instead, you can simply use a candle. Light a candle in front of you and sit in a calm and relaxing position. It is essential to be comfortable; otherwise, you will be distracted due to a lack of practice. Observe the fire for some time. Relax your breathing and calm your mind. Now, try to observe the surroundings of the fire. Imagine an energy circle surrounding it, growing and expanding its range. Lastly, imagine the circle bursting outward infinitely, creating waves of light energy again and again. Just like the sun, the outflow of energy is continuous and touches our skin. Imagine that the candlelight is similar to the sun, producing energy and radiating it around you. Feel that energy on your skin, as absorbing it is essential. Just as we have absorbed the Earth element, we are now focusing on absorbing the Fire element and connecting ourselves to the greatest source of fire, the sun, through the small flame of a candle.

Air element: The air element is tricky to truly consume because we constantly consume it without awareness. Right now, as you breathe, you are taking in air, likely without noticing it. Consuming air mindlessly nourishes the body but does not energise the spirit.

To engage fully with the air element, sit in a relaxed position and focus on your breath. Imagine inhaling fresh air from a serene valley or feeling a gentle ocean breeze. Visualise the air filling your chest, and expanding it as it enters. Hold your breath for a few moments and sense a surge of energy building within. Then exhale slowly, letting that energy radiate through your entire body.

Each breath can become more than a biological process. It becomes a way to connect with life itself. You no longer just take in air; you absorb vitality, calm, and clarity. The simple act of breathing transforms into an exchange with the world, allowing the energy of the air element to flow through you, rejuvenating both body and mind. Do not force yourself to do it quickly. Enjoy every breath you take and let its energy permeate your entire body. One good breath is better than 10 average ones. Focusing on the energy burst, then the flow, is key. Because of the nature of this element, you don't necessarily have to do it at home. You can also do it outside. For example, while walking towards your home or work, you see a beautiful tree or a plant. Stand there for a second and take a deep breath while looking at it. Imagine harnessing the energy surrounding it and using air to absorb it into your body.

Space element: unlike other elements, this needs to be done in a dark environment. You can close the light in the room and sit comfortably. Relax your mind and body. Take a few deep breaths and calm your nerves. Now, try to imagine the galaxy and the stars within it. The universe exists in space. There is no right or wrong imagination; it is yours. Once you can imagine the space, imagine yourself sitting in it. Imagine yourself as you are now, whether you look or feel like a godly character or not, focus on yourself. You are at the centre of the universe, sitting in the vastness of space. The goal is to increase the time you spend in that state. You don't actually consume this element, rather, you become one with it.

Remember, it is simply a technique along with its manual. You do not have to follow everything or expect the same experience. Creating your own experience is necessary. Your energy consumption may differ from that of your friend. There are various ways to consume energy. For instance, you can sit in a park, touch the grass, and feel the earth beneath it, experiencing similar sensations. Alternatively, you can visit a beach and dip your feet in the water, feeling the same physical sensations.

The key is to consume the positive energy from the elements and not how you consume it.

The release of energy

Osho paid the most attention to this aspect of life. However, some of his methods for teaching how to release energy are controversial. But the ideology behind them is worth considering.

Once you meditate regularly and become aware of the energies within you, you can consciously recognise and release the negative energy. Our body is like a jar and can only hold a certain amount of water. If you keep adding water, it will eventually overflow and spill everywhere. Similarly, our body can only store a limited amount of energy. Therefore, we must try to remove as much negative energy from it as possible; otherwise, it will spill.

There are multiple ways we can release our negative energy, and it is not rocket science. However, it appears difficult only because some people want it to be. For them to charge you money, it must be marketed as something complex and requiring special training.

It sounds simple to me, because it is. There are multiple ways to release energy, and one of the most common ways to do this is through aggressive activities that yield positive outcomes; for example, learning and practising the art of self-defence. Practising martial arts is an effective way to release negative energy, as it is rooted in aggression. You learn to fight, and you fight with your opponents. When you punch or kick, you release your negative energies. When you fight your opponent, you end up releasing your inner anger. You channel it in a way that it creates a positive impact. We all have negative energy within us, and if we do not release it, it will continue to build up and will be released onto someone we love. Therefore, we consciously release it in a way that creates a positive outcome, and martial arts is one of the best ways to do that.

Another way to release negative energy is through dancing. Now, you may not see anything aggressive with dancing, but there is. Regardless of the style, dancing involves the movement of hands and legs. To see how aggressive it actually is, we can do a simple exercise. Blindfold the dancer and ask them to continue dancing irrespective of what they hit. Now stand in front of the dancer, and you will realise how aggressive it can be. Dance is a form of expressing the aggression within. In Hinduism, there is a dance called the Shiv Tandav, which has two forms: Rudra Tandava, a destructive dance form that represents Shiva (the Hindu god) in his fierce, furious, and violent aspects. In contrast, Ananda Tandava signifies bliss and joy. Dancing helps us release our negative energy through vigorous movement, ultimately leading to a positive outcome.

Sex is another way to release negative energy, which leads to a positive outcome.

Before we discuss this further, I invite you to ask yourself a question. Do I act aggressively during sex? There could only be two answers: yes or no. If your answer is no and you are honest about it, then congratulations, you don't have much negative energy within you. However, if you are like most of us and your answer is yes, then don't stress. It is normal for one to be aggressive during sex. Now, before your mind starts telling you this is wrong – aggressiveness is not good, and it's not acceptable – let me describe sexual aggression. When two people are in love and consent to have sex, do they perform acts like scratching, pulling each other towards them with gentle force, biting, and talking to each other in a manner that they usually don't? Would you not call these acts of aggression?

Biting or scratching each other is not an act of aggression? Calling each other names to increase one's pleasure is not an act of aggression? Yes, it certainly is. However, what is the result of this act of aggression, one must ask? The answer is "Pleasure". Sex serves as a means to transform negative energies into thoughts, ultimately leading to a pleasurable outcome. What could be better than that? However, some people take this to an extreme through BDSM practices. I believe this is a personal choice, but the end result remains the same: releasing negative energy while achieving a positive outcome.

Sex is an act of significant controversy. Every guru, thinker, coach, priest, and monk has a different opinion on the matter. Every religion views it differently, and I don't want you to look at it through an orthodox lens or from a preconceived notion. You may look at a tree and see lumber, you may like to eat its fruit, you may want to sit under its shade, or you may simply like to observe its beauty from afar. How you look at something should be based on your understanding, not on someone else's.

By releasing the negative energies within us, we can maintain a balance of peace. This way, we won't be caught off guard by our emotions and will avoid sudden outbursts. Instead, we can fill ourselves with more positive energies, such as love and empathy.

WHAT IS GOD?

Discussing God and describing it is a book in itself. Therefore, I will keep it as concise as possible. In this section, I refer to God as "him" solely to ease the flow of reading. This is not meant to imply that God is male. You are free to address God in whatever way feels right to you.

Before we consider what God is, let's first examine our reasons for seeking to know God. Why do you want to understand or know God?

Is it because you want the answer to the most controversial question on earth? Or have you been searching for God for many years? Is it simply because you want to strengthen your beliefs? Or do you want to ask God 'why'?

I know that if your reason is strong enough to continue your pursuit, you will find God.

However, in reality, we all know God and have our own perceptions about Him. Try asking a Hindu what God is, and he will tell you their version of God and also describe what God looks like. Try asking a Christian, and he will have his own description of God. He will describe God as being all-knowing, powerful and loving. He will also tell you how to be near God and what things you should do to be closer to Him. Similarly, if you ask a Muslim, he, too, will have his own description of God and will tell you the means to be closer to God. Try asking a Buddhist about their perspective on God; you might be surprised by their interpretation and ideas on how to connect with the divine. Even if you ask five people from the same religion to share their beliefs about God, you will likely notice the differences in their perceptions. People of the same religion living in different countries will also have different perceptions of God. You can also find people who believe in the same God and share the same perception, yet have different understandings of the teachings.

Unlike other things in life, with God, we like to believe that there is only one correct answer. My perception of God is the correct one, and all the other perceptions are flawed. When it comes to God, people often refuse to compromise or even consider different perspectives. They are set in their beliefs, unwilling to hear anything that challenges what they have been told, even though their God has shown flexibility, patience, and compromise for the betterment of humanity.

There is no one answer to the question of what God is. Even if our world had only one religion, there would still be differences among its adherents. Therefore, how can there be only one answer?

I describe the concept of God in two ways. One, "God" itself, and the second, "Godly characteristics".

God

Anything that can produce and maintain life is God. Try to understand this with an open mind. "God" is a word used to refer to someone or something believed to be responsible for one's existence or for sustaining it.

Let's look at some common questions and the answers we often hear.

When asked, "Who created the first man and woman?" The answer is usually "God".

When asked, "Who created water, animals, and trees?" The answer is usually "God".

Ask yourself these questions, or, if you're an atheist, ask your friends.

When a believer asks, "How did we come into existence?" A scientist might reply, "Through the Big Bang."

The believer then responds, "And who created the Big Bang? There must be a God."

Let's consider both assumptions. First, if someone believes God created the Big Bang that formed the universe, then the existence of the Big Bang depends on God, correct? The other assumption is that the Big Bang created everything; the universe came into existence through it, and no external cause triggered it. Would it then be entirely wrong to call the Big Bang God itself?

Let's ask ourselves a question: who would a 1-day-old or even a 1-year-old child consider to be God—his or her mother, or the God we believe in? We have all heard the saying that we are all children of God. Is it possible that the mother was being referred to as "God" in this statement?

Let's take another example: think of an orphan child who was abandoned by his parents at the age of 3 and was sent to an orphanage which was funded by an old, wealthy lady. Now you must ask yourself, who is being a God to that child? The God we believe in or that old, wealthy lady. One can always justify by saying that God sent that old lady to help that poor child. But is that really so? If God sent that lady to help the child, then why did God decide to send only a few? Isn't our world filled with abandoned children and underfunded orphanages?

The point being, "God" is only a word, which we use to describe someone who either gives us life or helps us to maintain it.

Let me try to contradict this statement on your behalf. Here is an example to contradict this. Think of a family of four: husband, wife and two teenagers. The parents gave birth to them and now provide them with shelter, food, education, and unconditional love. Yet, many teenagers often speak unkindly to their parents, slam doors, and sometimes even harbour resentment towards them. So how can these parents be seen as God? Teenagers don't consider them as such, right?

Now, where have we heard a similar example before? I believe in a temple, or a church, or any other place of worship. The statement follows something like this: "You may choose not to follow God, but God will continue to take care of his children. He will always look after you, his children. He is merciful and will always accept you with open arms; he expects nothing but for you to be happy." Is it just me, or does this statement sound similar to the example we used with the teenagers, where parents took care of them unconditionally? Therefore, it is not wrong to use the term 'God' for someone or something that creates life and provides for it, even if that life chooses not to acknowledge its existence.

Just as we drink water every day, we rarely consider the water itself. We do not think about where the water is coming from or what it is. We use it for our own existence without being thankful for it. Similarly, one could be a God, but may not be considered so.

"God" is a simple word, but a mighty one. The word "God" carries hope within it, which is the hope of nourishment and safety. A hope that can also be found in mothers and fathers and even nature itself. However, this hope is not exclusive to humans; it applies to all living creatures. A mother elephant protects her calf, feeds it until it matures, and teaches lessons essential for survival. To the baby elephant, its mother is its 'God', the one who provides nourishment, protection, and a sense of safety. If God created everything, then He created animals as well. He must be a God to them, too, one who protects and loves them. It would be narrow-minded to believe that God exists only for human beings. If He exists, then He must exist for all. We must ask ourselves: what is the definition of God from the perspective of animals? Someone who came from heaven solely to care for humanity? Or someone who provides nourishment, safety, and guidance for the survival of every being?

I am not denying the existence of the Gods we all believe in, but I am asking you to take a different perspective, to see them in a new light.

We must understand that the nature around us is a reflection of God. How? Because without it, our parents would not have survived, and we would have never been born to discuss and read about all of this. If any element of nature ceases to exist today, we will all die of hunger or of a natural calamity, and there will be no one left to visit a temple or church.

It would not be wrong to call our parents God, and our parents to call theirs God. We can all consider nature (including water, air, plants, animals, and more) as a representation of God. Nature can call our planet God. The Earth can call its solar system God. The solar system can consider the universe as God, and the universe can recognise the Big Bang as its God.

The point is that the word 'God' can be used in many ways, and this is one of the main reasons why different religions exist in the world.

You can see this in history: the Greeks used to attribute various aspects of life and nature as Gods. They named their Gods after thunder, ocean, lightning, and more. Why did they do that? Because they believed that rain, lightning, and water were essential to their survival and that without them they would cease to exist. And in many ways, that is true. So they called these forces Gods. As our civilisation developed further and we gained a deeper understanding of our world and universe, we created new Gods. Many civilisations began worshipping the planets and calling them Gods, such as the Sun God or the Moon Goddess. Now we know for a fact that without the sun, our planet will freeze to death, and life will cease to exist. Therefore, would you call those people wrong for calling the sun their God? Let's rewind a few thousand years. We were looking at the sky and asking ourselves questions: what's beyond the stars? Who created these stars? And we began to question things we did not understand at the time; also, we didn't have advanced science to answer those questions. So we started to believe in the all-powerful invisible God who created the universe.

As I stated previously, anything that can produce life and sustain it is called God. This includes animals, plants and natural elements. However, humans possess something unique compared to other beings. As humans, we can exhibit and display various characteristics. On the other hand, animals are limited in their abilities. Animals are less capable than humans. Their mental and physical characteristics bind them. However, despite these limitations, people in the past have referred to animals, even rivers and mountains as Gods. A prime example of this can be seen in India. Where people still worship cows as God. This is a concept that is challenging to understand for Western society. However, aside from the mythology, the most likely explanation is that cows were considered important livestock. People in India have been and still are highly dependent on their livestock for survival. Milk and its related products, such as curd, cheese, and butter, remain an essential part of their diet. This strong dependence on an animal for survival led them to regard cows as God.

In ancient times, many civilisations considered different animals to be Gods. The primary reason behind this is population. Imagine a world with only a few humans, where animals dominate. A world where humans fear wild animals and rely on their mercy for survival. They worship animals and ask them for their protection. However, the ability of humans to attain and portray Godly characteristics makes them the most ideal candidate to be called God. Humans can not only protect, care and help their own species but also others. This might be true of other beings as well, but the point of differentiation lies in the intention. A river may provide life and support to animals living near it, but it does so unintentionally. Only humans can provide intentionally; we can take care of ourselves while helping other living beings in need. This leads to our current understanding of the concept of God.

When we examine the various religions of the world, we find many different Gods, but what's fascinating is that these diverse Gods share similar divine characteristics. Isn't that something worth understanding? Different Gods having similar characteristics: how and what?

Godly characteristics

Godly characteristics are what make humans godlike. This may sound unusual at first, but before judging whether the statement is true or false, it is worth examining these qualities more closely. So what are they? Awareness, empathy, and selflessness. These traits elevate us and set us apart. They are what make us different and what transform a human into something godlike.

When I use the word "God", I do not mean an immortal being with supernatural powers. Everything that exists will one day perish. I am referring instead to the capacity to nurture, create, and sustain life. One might ask why it is necessary to describe these characteristics when God has already been defined. The reason is simple: humans possess the ability to create and sustain life within their surroundings. We are capable of selflessness, a quality not shared by all living beings, and we process the world in a way that is distinct from other forms of life.

All three of these characteristics are common in whichever God one chooses to worship.

All Gods have demonstrated tremendous selflessness, empathy for others, and total awareness of themselves and their surroundings. These are the things that made them different from the rest of us. But these are not the characteristics one is born with. One can develop or embed them into one's life over time. Does that mean we can all be God? That would not be totally wrong. But it is easier said than done. To possess these characteristics and live by them is a highly challenging task. A task that could potentially require a lifetime or sometimes even more. Let's look at these characteristics in more detail.

Complete awareness

A significant amount of knowledge about awareness comes from Buddhism and from the teachings of Gautama Buddha. If you learn about Buddhism and become more familiar with the Buddha himself, you will soon realise that awareness is one of its central ideologies. To be fully aware of one's actions, be aware of every single aspect of your being. To be completely awake and not asleep, even when asleep. In total awareness, you must be aware of your every movement. If you move your hand, you move it knowingly. If you are walking, you should be aware; every step you take should be intentional.

When you are eating, you should be fully aware of every action involved in the eating process. Being aware of your hand when picking up the food, your eyes when you see the food, your nose when you smell the food, and your mouth when you chew the food. The concept of awareness is singular, meaning it discourages multitasking and encourages doing one thing at a time, with awareness. Even things you might consider wrong or sinful, you should do with awareness, as awareness will help you realise their taste and make a sound decision to continue or stop them.

Being aware of ourselves, our thoughts, and what's within us is something we often hear about when reading about meditation or practising it. But how many of us actually know what it means to be aware of our thoughts? Being aware of your thoughts means not dismissing any thoughts that come to mind without holding and thinking about them.

According to science, we experience over thirty thousand thoughts every day. So, how can we be aware of all of them and pause to think about them individually? The process seems impossible. It is, but only if you think of them as just thoughts. We have discussed before that thoughts are energy in conversion. If we control our energy consumption, we will have fewer, and more positive thoughts, making it easier for us to focus and concentrate. Now, do you know why monks and yogis can meditate for so long, and you can't? Because they have limited thoughts as they consciously consume or absorb their energies. It is not that they are special and you are not; it is because they are more aware of their surroundings and themselves than we are. If you start connecting all the dots, it will all make sense, and the confusion will leave your mind.

If you have a positive thought, you need to stop and ask yourself: What caused me to think this way, and why do I keep doing those things more often? In other words, consume more of that particular positive energy. If you have a negative thought, then ask yourself, 'Why do I feel this way?' What is causing me to think badly about others? Or why am I feeling jealous? Is it because of something I consumed, such as spending time with people who are envious of others, and I consumed their energy? Once you are totally aware of yourself, you feel not only at peace but also stable.

Being aware is like being a large rock that is lying in the middle of a flowing river, with water moving effortlessly around it. Similarly, by cultivating full awareness, you develop a sense of stability that allows life's problems and worries to pass through you without disturbing your inner calm. Awareness does not stop the river of life, but it keeps you grounded, steady, and unshaken amidst its currents. It is a state that can be seen in many of our Gods. If you study their characters deeply enough, you will find this to be true. Therefore, to reach a higher state, we should aim for total awareness. Most of us who practice meditation or follow religious teachings are partially aware. However, to be fully aware, it takes continuous practice, time and patience.

Awareness brings freedom to oneself, and complete awareness brings freedom to others. In the state of complete awareness, there is no sleep, only awakening. Even when you are asleep, you are aware of your dreams. You see your thoughts flowing in front of you. You can stop and understand them. You can realise what energy created that thought, and can have complete control over it. To be in control of your thoughts is to be in control of yourself. In total awareness, sleep becomes what it is meant to be: rest for your body and nothing else. The mind never sleeps; if it did, then there wouldn't be any dreams. As you become more and more aware, you realise the unnecessary actions you do and thoughts you create. To be in a state of complete awareness is like having the sun shining for 24 hours a day. You can always see things clearly—a characteristic fit for a God.

Complete selflessness

We have heard this word many times. Selflessness, as the word describes, is an act of doing something for others without any self-interest. We all have heard about it, but only a few have truly understood it. Helping a blind man cross the road or rescuing an injured animal are examples we often use to define selflessness. We refer to such examples as acts of selflessness. So, is there any other definition of selflessness? For someone who wants to live an everyday life, then no. But if you want to go deeper and higher, then it's a yes.

We call ourselves selfless, but we should also ask ourselves: do we expect happiness in return for our act of kindness? When we help a blind man cross the road, do we expect a thank you in the end? Or when we go home and tell our friends and family about the incident, does it make us feel good? Do we expect love from the animals we rescued? I am not saying that helping someone is not a good thing in itself; it is, and in fact, a marvellous thing. However, expecting even the faintest happiness in return for kindness can hinder your state of complete selflessness. If you look at selflessness from a different perspective, you will see that every act of kindness has a condition until it becomes a complete act of selflessness. In the state of complete selflessness, one becomes indifferent to the outcome of the act. For example, if you help someone without a personal motive and that person swears at you in return, will you feel bad? Or will you stop being selfless? If such incidents continue, will you still act selflessly? The act of complete selflessness is a Godly characteristic because, with complete selflessness, one continues to perform acts of selflessness even in the face of a negative response.

Jainism talks about penance and detachment. However, if we understand the teachings of Mahavira, we will see a state of complete selflessness. Some of the teachings recorded in ancient texts suggest that one should be detached from everything; some believers still follow this path. They choose to abandon everything, including their clothes and any other worldly belongings. They walk barefoot, have no clothes on their backs, and eat only specific foods. They follow the path of Mahavira to its core and try to replicate his lifestyle. The only reason Mahavira lived this way was that he had attained the state of complete selflessness. Abounding in materialistic things and consuming only what is required for the survival of the body is an act of complete selflessness. Where one wants nothing for himself and sacrifices everything for others. No matter which God you believe in, they all have attained complete selflessness. Most of them sacrificed themselves for others or dedicated their entire lives to serving others. While their methods of service might have varied, the underlying approach was similar.

Offering what you have in abundance, whether wealth, time, or power, may be generous, but it does not reflect absolute selflessness. Giving what you need most, or what you have in limited supply, is the essence of selflessness. Even dogs care for their puppies. Then what makes us special if you take care of your kids? True selflessness is when you care more about orphans than your own children. My intention here is not to make you feel bad or to tell you that you are not doing well enough, but to show you what God did, and if you really want to follow in the footsteps of God, then what should be done.

Being completely selfless is extremely difficult, and

possessing godly characteristics is not meant to be easy. True selflessness demands conscious effort, sacrifice, and the willingness to place something beyond oneself at the centre of one's actions. It often requires giving up comfort, convenience, and even personal gain. This is precisely why such qualities are rare and revered. If being godly were easy, it would be common.

Complete empathy

Empathy is a unique Godly characteristic. It lies between the line of complete selflessness and complete awareness. We use the word 'empathy' as a joke these days. Empathy is a profound characteristic and not easy to come by. It's a double-edged sword, one that is not easy to wield. Empathy comes with pain and hurt. We all empathise, don't we? But on a surface level. We look at a differently abled child and say, "Oh, poor him or her!" We feel bad for a few seconds or minutes, then go back to our daily lives.

Let's look at another example. We all have had salespeople on our doorstep, haven't we? And how many times do we open the door and talk to them nicely? Not many times, correct? Ask yourself this question: Do we empathise with them? Sales jobs are difficult, and door-to-door even more so. These people get sworn at, have a door shut in their face and are even threatened sometimes. To have empathy means to ask yourself, 'Why would someone do a job like that?' What are the circumstances that made them choose this career? Please understand, I am not saying this for you to start buying everything a salesman sells, but to put yourself in their shoes before being unkind to them.

Being nice to someone is not as hard as we think, but being nice to someone who is being rude to you is. I am not talking about being nice to them just on the surface, but about being genuinely nice to them from the heart. If someone screams at you for no reason, do you respond back in anger or silence, or do you think to yourself that they might be having a terrible day or going through a tough time? You may argue that in today's world, many people are rude and lack basic courtesy, and that you should not feel empathy toward them. That is acceptable if one chooses to live an ordinary, everyday life, and there is nothing inherently wrong with it. However, this cannot be called complete empathy. True empathy does not discriminate between a man who is paralysed and a man who goes door to door selling goods, or between the rude and the kind.

Another factor that makes empathy difficult to achieve is its counterpart. When we see sadness and pain in someone else, we feel them in ourselves. We intentionally consume and absorb energy. I have heard stories about mystics and Gods who touched people and took their pain and suffering as their own, helping them. Now I don't think it is possible at a physical level, but it is possible at a spiritual level. A prominent example of this can be seen in Christianity, where Jesus died to atone for our sins. As mentioned in 1 Peter 2:24a, "He Himself bore our sins in His body on the cross, that we might die to sin and live to righteousness." My understanding of this phrase is that Jesus, who was sinless himself, sacrificed himself willingly and took the sins of all humanity upon himself. This is an act of complete empathy, as Jesus did not discriminate against humanity in carrying their sins. He took the sins of all – poor, rich, old, young, healthy, deceased, good and bad. Thus, I call complete empathy a Godly characteristic. To be empathetic, you may have to sacrifice your peace, happiness, time, or sometimes even yourself. Complete empathy is not easy, as it liberates others. By being empathetic, you can liberate others from their sadness, suffering, and pain, and sometimes even from their sins.

One sentence

If I have to summarise everything written above in one line, then it would be:

"All humans are born God, and all Gods are born human."

This means that all of us have the potential to be like Gods by developing our Godly characteristics, and all Gods were born like us. I don't think Gods were born with special abilities or powers. Yet they gained them through their curiosity, through their knowledge of self and others, through seeking and asking the right questions and, most importantly, by practising. If Gods were sent from heaven or clouds, then they must all have looked the same, possessed the same powers, and shared the same beliefs, perhaps with some different teachings, but mostly the same. But that did not happen. Every God we know of or have heard of is different from the other. I am not denying the existence of God; I believe in the existence of every God and praise their teachings. But I don't think they came from above us; I think they came from among us.

WHAT IS THE SOUL?

Before you ask yourself, or anyone else, questions about the soul, such as: Is there one? What is it? What happens to it? What does it look like? And how do I connect with it? I encourage you to do this one thing first.

Think of the most essential piece of technology you use every day, and the one you cannot imagine your life without anymore. For most of us, it would be our mobile phone. Most of us spend hours using it every day; we buy protective cases, clean it, charge it, use it to connect with people, do work-related tasks, and engage in many recreational activities. It is undoubtedly a vital and valuable tool for us, and surviving without it seems almost impossible today.

Before you start questioning my sanity and the relevance of discussing a phone while talking about the soul, ask yourself a few questions. For example, what colour are the wires within my phone? What colour chip is powering my phone? How does the electric current run from the battery to the chipboard to the LED screen? Or how did engineers design the technology to make the phone touchscreen?

These are all relevant questions, aren't they? We must at least understand the basics of one of the most valuable aspects of our existence. How does it look? How does it work? How was it created?

You should be familiar with these ideas before delving into the concept of the soul. And why is this important? Because our bodies are not fundamentally different from mobile phones. It is intelligent, composed of multiple elements, requires recharging, needs maintenance, helps us perform tasks, and eventually stops working.

Think about your phone for a moment. Is knowing that it has the latest chip, a strong battery, and a good camera enough to use it effectively and improve your life? Or do you really need to know the exact colour of the wires inside before using it?

The point is this: why waste time and energy trying to understand something that is not immediately useful to you? Knowing every detail might benefit the company that manufactures the device, but it will not make your life any easier. You use the phone to communicate, organise, create, and be productive, not to dismantle it and analyse every component.

Similarly, let God or whatever you believe in take care of the workings of the soul, its connection to the body, or even its colour. Your focus should be on utilising your body and mind to live a good and productive life, rather than spending decades trying to locate or define the soul. Even if you could discover it, what practical use would it serve? You cannot hold it, capture it, touch it, or directly apply it in your daily life.

Searching for the soul is like buying a new phone, opening it up, and spending months or years trying to understand every single part and the technology behind it. What would you achieve? Perhaps a sense of superiority in knowledge, but at what cost? While dissecting it, you would likely abandon the device's usefulness and productivity.

Now, some critical thinkers might point out that a phone repair technician knows every part of a phone and even the colour of the wires. That is true, but do they know how the chip is manufactured? What materials go into the battery, the camera, or the screen? Probably not. They know where each component belongs and how to replace it, but not its full construction or origin. To truly know every detail, one would likely have to change professions, study multiple disciplines, and even then would not have complete knowledge of every element that went into building the device.

The same principle applies to the soul. Spending your life chasing its secrets while neglecting the body and mind is largely unproductive. This is similar to some spiritual gurus who claim to know the colour of your soul, how it was created, and other intricate details. While such knowledge may be fascinating, it rarely helps you live a better, more meaningful life.

The real question is not what the soul is, but why you want to know. What do you hope to achieve by discovering it? True usefulness comes from mastering the body and mind, understanding yourself, and using your faculties to improve your life and the lives of those around you. That is the practical, actionable pursuit of being human.

Coming back to the original question about what a soul is? If you still want to know, I must tell you there is no single answer. Unlike God, no one knows if it really exists and if it does, what it is. To me, the soul is a matter of insignificance. If it exists, great, and if it doesn't, that's good too. However, if you're seeking a definitive answer to satisfy your curiosity, then the soul is essentially whatever your spiritual leaders, holy scriptures, or the monks and thinkers you follow say it is.

Believe in all that they tell you. The soul is energy. The soul is eternal. Souls transfer from one body to another. The soul goes to heaven and hell. And also, there is no such thing as a soul.

You should not waste your life and energy searching for it or trying to understand it. Let God take care of the manufacturing, and you focus on being useful. Otherwise, you will waste your life while figuring it out, unless you have the desire to become a creator of souls.

WHY ME?

There is no one correct answer to this question. Many have asked this question and tried to answer it, but they are all right and wrong at the same time. To answer the question 'Why me?' we have to understand life, and the answer will present itself to you. I said there is no single correct answer because my understanding of life may differ from yours. Therefore, my answer to 'Why me?' might differ from yours. Let's try to understand this "Why me?" Haven't we all asked this question at some stage in our lives? We all have heard of statements like, 'Why only me?' and 'Why is this happening to me?' It is interesting to note that these statements are often used in a negative context. We blame life for all our misshapenness. Isn't it true? How many times have we heard people say, "I was able to participate in this race because of my efforts." Or "I achieved this because of what I did." We have made it our nature to take credit for our wins and blame life for our losses. I find this behaviour hypocritical. We should either take credit for both our losses and wins, or give life the credit for the same. The question 'Why me?' is not only limited to losses but also to life in general. Why am I sent to this world? Why am I like this? There are many more aspects.

For most of us, the "me" is easy to understand. However, the life part is still mysterious. When we say, 'Why did this happen to me?' We are referring to life or God. Statements like, 'God did this to me,' or 'Why does God not like me?' It is what we usually get confused with, as we are never able to find the answer. You can't find the answer by blaming; you can only hope to find the answer by trying to understand the situation.

The best way to understand life is through a game of chess. Life is like a game of chess in which there is you and the opponent. The opponent can be called life itself. The moment you make your first conscious choice, the game starts. If it is the right move, you win; otherwise, life wins. Now we all know one move does not decide the game. We continue making our choices until either you or life reaches checkmate. A checkmate for you is dying with regret, sadness and desires, and a checkmate for life is you dying with happiness, satisfaction and contentment.

Every move or conscious choice we make allows life to counter it. There is no prediction of how the game would look at any single point. We go through the entire game to see how one played. Just like a game of chess, if you have practised making the right move, the game will be short, and you will have the chance to win. Or if you are one of those who have no understanding of the game, it could take you a very long time. Your moves will be slow, and you will eventually be defeated. Now imagine if you have reached the end and are about to give a checkmate to life. Would you ask this question, "Why me?" Or why did I win?" I believe you won't. Why? Because you know you made all the right moves. Similarly, in real life, we make decisions in order to win. These decisions become righteous when guided by self-knowledge, which some may call goodness or the path of God.

Let's answer the question: *Why me,* using a different example. You must have heard of the domino effect. If not, it can be defined as a chain reaction in which one event triggers a series of subsequent, related events. Life is like a domino effect. The first domino is the smallest but the hardest to move, and the last domino is the largest and takes literally no effort to fall.

In life, we find ourselves at the end of a domino chain, where our emotions can sway between happiness and sadness. If we push the first domino with positive energy and make the right choices, it sets off a chain reaction, sending larger and larger dominoes our way. This process continues until the largest domino of happiness falls upon us. For example, if you teach your child good deeds and to be gentle and humble towards others, the child will grow up to be a good human being and will probably take care of you when you are 80 years old. He or she probably won't put you in an old-age home and meet you more than once a year. The full effect of that first domino you pushed may not be realised at first, but by the time you are hit by the last, you will know.

The same goes for the negative, and the effects are far worse. If you push the first domino with negative energy, by the time the last one hits, you will be saying, 'Why me?' For example, if you drink alcohol in front of your children, you sometimes give them a spoon or two to help them sleep quickly. There is a very high probability that your child will grow up to be an alcoholic, and you will have a miserable life ahead. I am not against drinking, but I am just making you aware that what you do today may affect you tomorrow. If you disagree with this example, then you should join an AL-ANON meeting once.

Let us look at another example: how the first domino is pushed. If you choose to flirt with one of your colleagues, it may seem harmless at first. Like the first domino, it takes effort to push, and its effect is not immediately visible. However, if the flirting continues, there is a strong possibility it will lead to an affair, whether with that person or someone else.

Today, even an affair may appear normal to some, but it can carry serious consequences in the future. If you are married, it may lead to divorce; your partner may take half of your possessions, and you could even end up on the streets. This is often the moment when people ask, "Why me?" They blame God, life, and everything around them, except their own actions. When the last domino is about to fall, there is very little left to do but wait and watch it happen. What began as simple flirting five years ago ends in ruin today.

This principle is not limited to personal relationships. It applies to every aspect of life. Even in business, a single wrong decision made long ago can one day lead to bankruptcy.

Life is like having multiple chains of dominoes—the energy you use to push the first one matters. If you believe that whatever wrong that has happened to you or is happening to you is the work of God or destiny, then you should also give complete credit for your wins to God or destiny, not partial.

Now, some things are beyond the domino effect. Things that we don't control. For example, what kind of parents do we get? Or if you were born healthy or with a disability? You do not cause these events, but they have a significant effect on you. This is probably the most challenging part of life to understand. The 'why?' To answer this, people have used words like 'faith', 'destiny', 'past life karma', 'act of God' or simply 'luck'. It doesn't matter what you call it; we spend our energy, sometimes our entire life, just to name it. Naming it is not the important part here; understanding and accepting it is more important. For instance, if you go on a wildlife safari and encounter an animal you have never seen before, your first question will be, "What is this?" followed by an appreciation of its beauty and features. You would not be overly concerned with its name. If your tour guide tells you that the animal is a "jaguar," when in reality it is a leopard, you would likely accept it without question and move on. Similarly, for centuries, we have been fighting to name things we don't know instead of finding out what they are. If you put two scholars of different religions together, then there is a very high probability that they will end up fighting over names and only pointing out what they think is wrong in the other person's religion. What they should do instead is to share their thoughts and understanding of their own religion and its teachings, and also try to understand what the other religion teaches.

To understand the uncontrollable aspects of life, we must first accept that there are things we simply cannot understand. The key here is to understand the difference between events caused by your own actions and those that occur naturally. To understand this, we need to be honest with ourselves and engage in introspection. If our own actions cause it, then we take responsibility and try to do better next time. If it's caused by something outside our control, good or bad, then we must simply accept it. If you attend a school and one of your teachers is not good, do you leave the school? You can either complain or merely accept it and wait till you graduate to the next class. Similarly, if you get a great teacher for one subject, will you skip all the other classes and attend only that one?

Life is such; there are things you can and cannot change. To answer the 'Why me?' question, we see life, understand its various aspects, change some, and accept others. If we can do this successfully, then we won't ask this question, as we will be satisfied with our understanding. The question of what life is will transform into life itself.

WHAT IS DEATH?

Death, my friend, is the most beautiful thing in this world. And it is ironic how much we fear it. It is like graduating or finishing the class you desperately wanted to end. Now you may say, 'What if I loved the class?' You might have, but imagine studying in the same class you loved for 60, 70 or sometimes 90 years. Would you still love it just as much? You must enjoy the class and learn a lot from it, and that's it. Close the book, pack your bag and leave. Death is exactly like that. One doesn't mind the class getting over, so why mind death? Perhaps because you can no longer attend the class?

I have heard people, specifically men, who would give anything to be back in class with their friends. Why is that? Because they had fun. Can they not have it now?

Death originates from birth, so would it be wrong to say that death is the closest thing to birth? If we agree to that concept, it would not be wrong to say that a newborn child is closest to death, as he was dead or non-existent before being alive or coming into this world. It came out of death/non-existence and was born into this world of ours. Someone who has experienced death and birth so closely would surely be fearful. But are they? Does a child think about death? Or cares that he might die tomorrow or maybe someday. If the baby who has experienced it closely doesn't care about it, then why do we?

Death can be complex, but it can also be straightforward. It depends on us and what we make of it. Should we enjoy the journey or ruin it by thinking of the destination? The decision is ours.

We die every day, yet we fear the end. Suppose we have a bowl full of fruit and we start eating one piece at a time. We don't think about the fruit finishing when we take the first bite, but midway, we begin to realise that it will be over soon. When there are only a few pieces of fruit left in the bowl, we really start to panic and wish we hadn't wolfed it down, or maybe should have savoured the taste a bit more.

However, if we get a bowl of fruit and decide not to eat it because of our fear of finishing it, we often forget that the fruit will eventually rot by itself. It is in one's best interest to eat the fruit because the bowl will be empty one way or another.

We focus too much on the result, which is beyond our control, and forget to enjoy the process.

So what exactly happens when one dies? Is there reincarnation? Or does the soul go to heaven or hell? Or is there simply nothing after we die? Death is a great question, but is it really that relevant? We must ask ourselves.

However, for the sake of understanding, it is essential to explore this further. No matter what religion you follow, everything that has been told to you about death and what happens after that is absolutely accurate and incorrect at the same time.

This statement unsettles the mind. How can all of it

be true? If truth is singular, how can it appear in multiple, conflicting forms? And if something is true, in what sense can it also be false?

Do we reincarnate? Do we go to heaven or hell? Or is there absolutely nothing after death? There can be only one right answer, correct? But what if they all are correct?

Let's understand this further; for example, consider the following statement: "Milk is used for making cheese." Ask yourself if this is a true statement. Before reading this further, say the following statement, "Milk is used for making cheese," to a few people around you while conversing and listen to their responses.

These are some of the most common things you will hear.

1. Some will agree and say yes, it's true. Milk is used to make cheese, and the type of milk used is specifically selected to produce the finest cheese.
2. Some will say, 'Yes, it is true milk is used to make cheese, but it could be used to make many other edible items and can also be used as an ingredient in some of the dishes.'
3. Some people will say that milk is excellent and that you should drink it every day for good health.
4. Some will say, 'I don't know if it's any good because I am lactose intolerant and it makes me sick.'
5. A vegan person might say it's nothing but animal cruelty. You should not use it.

Now, what do you think about the statement, "Milk is used to make cheese"? Isn't it a correct statement? Then how is it possible to have different interpretations of an accurate statement? Can it not carry multiple meanings? It can be both true and false, depending on the situation and the people involved. Similarly, what happens after death is true and untrue at the same time. It depends on how we understand it and what it means to us.

Death is one, but it has many meanings and forms. While all of them are true, all of them are false. It depends on what you believe in. Because if you don't believe in something, it automatically becomes false.

Let's focus on the three most popular ideologies of death and what happens to us after we die, as per them.

First, the concept of reincarnation.

Second, the concept of hell and heaven.

Third, the concept of nothingness.

Concept of reincarnation

The concept of reincarnation is ancient, originating in India, and is still believed by billions of people today. According to this belief, a person's soul is transferred into a new body based on the karma they have accumulated in a previous life. It is firmly based on karma, which means doing. If one's karma is good in this life, one shall be born into a good family in the next life, and if one's karma is bad, one shall be born into a lower form of life, such as a dog or an insect. The next life is dependent on the current one. And the cycle continues, and there is no death. One is reborn into a new life after death based on one's karma. Death is simply the door to a new life. The soul remains immortal and continually changes bodies, just as one changes old clothes.

This concept may or may not make sense depending on

your circumstances, such as your region, culture or religion. However, let's consider this from a broader perspective and with a different angle.

If one assumes that they are simply a body, and there is no such thing as reincarnation. Then what happens when they die? One is simply buried or burnt, and ashes are scattered. Let's look at this phenomenon more closely. What happens when one is dead and buried? The body begins to decompose, and most of it transforms into soil and compost. What happens to it after 10 years or 100 years? Things start to grow on it, whether it's grass or a tree. Then what happens to that grass or tree? Some animals might eat it. Any animal could eat it; it could be a rabbit or a deer.

Now, do you remember what we discussed about energy and how we consume it? We consume energy from what we eat, and that's true for both humans and animals. The vibration or energy doesn't die; it is either transferred or changes form. Could it be then said that the body's energy transforms into soil, which then transfers its energy to grass? Finally, when an animal consumes the grass, it carries some of your energy or vibrations.

If you think carefully, this process of transferring and consumption of energy and vibrations is similar to the concept of reincarnation in many ways. One may not become an animal in the next life, but could be living within one?

Concept of Hell and Heaven

It is the most common and widely accepted concept around the world, shared by many religions and cultures. In this belief, those who do wrong in their lives go to hell, where they are punished according to their actions. Those who live rightly and follow the teachings given to them go to heaven, a place of immense beauty and pleasure.

Similar to the concept of reincarnation, one may choose not to believe in Heaven and Hell. However, these ideas may still hold true from certain perspectives. For example, imagine a person in a sinking boat in the middle of an ocean. They drown, and shortly after, their body is torn apart by fish. Is that not a form of hell? Let's consider another scenario: a person dies and is buried in a forest. After a few hundred years, a tree grows above them, perhaps one that bears fruit, provides shade, and becomes home to countless birds. Would that not be a kind of heaven for many life forms? In a way, how one dies could mirror heaven or hell. Being buried in a peaceful cemetery among loved ones, with family visiting and leaving flowers, feels like heaven to me. Dying an unmarked, forgotten death in a distant desert feels no less than hell.

So, what is the concept of heaven and hell? Is it accurate or not?

The concept of nothingness

Nothingness is a concept primarily used by individuals who don't believe in God or by adherents of a specific religion or faith. The idea of nothingness is the most debatable one. It is used by many to contradict the above two. People who believe in nothingness often say things like, 'Have you seen God? How do you know for sure that you will go to heaven? Has anyone ever returned from the dead to describe what lies beyond it?' The concept of nothingness is that you cease to exist as soon as you die. There is nothing beyond that. A beautiful concept that eliminates much confusion. Or does it simply allow you to do whatever you want to do without caring about the consequences?

Let's examine nothingness through the same lens we used for reincarnation and heaven or hell.

Imagine a woman on a desert safari. Her car breaks down, leaving her stranded in the middle of the desert, where she eventually dies. What do you think will happen? The body will decompose, and after that? Nothing. There are no trees, and very few animals. What would happen to her energy? The energy will transfer to the sand. There is nothing beyond that, no consumption and no further transfer of energy. The desert may remain unchanged for a 1,000 years or even longer. What would you call such a death, and what would become of it? There would be no further transfer of energy.

If one doesn't believe in God or in energy, then the philosophy of death has no meaning at all, making life, in that sense, simpler to live.

Letter to death

It doesn't matter how you die; if you die with a smile on your face, then you died well. If you have lived a happy and fulfilled life, no matter which religion you belong to or what God you believe in, whether it's hell or nirvana you reach after you die, it will hold no impact on your current life. So why should you die thinking about death, and what will happen after that? We already struggle to manage our current lives, including our jobs, partners, and children, yet we often worry about controlling what will happen to us after we die. Instead, let's focus on the present. The only reason to discuss death in such detail is to come to terms with it.

Hear everything that is being told to you, but listen to only what is required. Do not die today with the worry of dying tomorrow.

What Jesus said was true, what Krishna said was true, what Buddha said was true, and whatever any other God said is also true. If the destination is the moon, you can reach it from any country. You can launch from the United States, the UK, China, or India. The rocket may take off from anywhere in the world, but the destination remains the same.

I once heard a saying that the only difference between your religion and mine is one. If there are 10 religions or Gods, I don't believe in 9, and neither do you. If you believe in the 1 that I believe in, then we both don't believe in the other 9. Similarly with death, the only difference is 1. If I believe in nothingness and you believe in hell or heaven, and we both don't believe in reincarnation or anything else that may happen after death, then the only difference between us is of 1.

We must accept death as we accept the air we breathe. Death is a necessary means to our survival, just like air is. Imagine a world where no one dies. What would happen? The population would continue to grow, and the Earth's resources would eventually dwindle. This could lead to a future filled with starving and desperate individuals, all begging for an end. Therefore, for a viable future to be possible, death plays a critical role. So, why is such an essential phenomenon viewed so negatively? It is simply due to our short-sightedness and nothing more.

We must say this every day: I am happy to die with a smile on my face and contentment in my heart. I accept and cherish all aspects of life, both good and bad, including birth and death.

WHAT IS MONEY?

Before we finish our journey of knowing, there is one last thing that must be discussed (money). A subject that is largely absent or regarded as unworthy of attention by most thinkers, scholars, spiritual leaders, and religious traditions. Money is often viewed as something to be avoided and is frequently associated with greed and evil. Money is often discussed as an obstacle that hinders one's attainment of enlightenment. The Buddha left his kingdom, his wealth, and his prosperity to live as a bhikshu (a person who is disconnected from all social aspects of the world). He walked barefoot and asked for food to feed himself. Although I have nothing against the path he chose, it was a different time altogether.

If you try to live that way and go door to door asking for food. What do you think will happen? Try walking barefoot and living in a forest to see what happens. This could be a way of living, but unfortunately, most of us were not taught to be monks or the importance of enlightenment, which comes from renouncing everything one holds dear. Most of us were taught about language, history, science, and math, with the ultimate motive of earning money and providing for our families.

We spend 20-25 years learning to become capable of

earning money and providing for our families. However, when we face difficulties in life and look to great minds, sacred texts, or religions for guidance, we are often told that we must renounce everything, and only then will we be happy. Now ask yourself: would it solve your problem or create more confusion? Something we've devoted most of our lives to suddenly becomes a problem. Everything we were taught—studying hard, building careers, striving for success—is now labelled as harmful, said to lead to desire, greed, and deceit. So what should we do with this contradiction? Blame our parents? Blame our schools? That would definitely solve everything… right?

You must know that no one in this world could survive more than a month without money or without relying on someone who has it. So, is it acceptable for someone to avoid earning money and depend on another person who has money? Isn't there a double standard? You must think and ask yourself.

So what is there to know about money? We are all familiar with it and desire it. So what's wrong with that? Nothing. Then why have so many religions looked down upon it? Why do spiritual gurus treat it as a bad thing? There must be a reason. After all, people kill for money, lie for it, cheat for it, gamble for it, and sometimes even marry for it. So does that make money officially "bad"? Before deciding whether something is good or bad, you must understand it thoroughly and examine it from different perspectives. Just as there is heaven and hell, with earth in between… Just as there is good and evil, with humans living in the middle… similarly, there are three types of money: good money, bad money, and essential money.

Let's understand the difference between good money, essential money and bad money.

Good money is when you earn money not only for your own survival but also for the betterment of others. One can be motivated to earn more money not only to provide for their own family but also to support other selfless causes. It could be helping orphans, protecting wildlife, or simply planting more trees. A reason that is simply selfless. You may argue that I am a business owner, and I pay salaries to many staff, helping them support their families. But is it truly selfless? You must ask. No business runs without employees. A business without employees is no business at all. It's a two-way street: they work, and you pay. It is important what you do with your money.

If you want to do good and pursue a higher, more selfless goal, you must earn more money, as it is good money.

Let's look at another example to clarify the concept further. Imagine there are two kings: one who thinks only about power and money. He enjoys all the riches in life and doesn't care much about his subjects. The other king is very content with what he has and keeps his subjects happy, encouraging their learning and development. Now ask yourself, who should earn more money? Sadly, the evil king continues to conquer more kingdoms and grows richer, while the good king decides to leave everything behind and follow the path of self-awareness. The question is, who should have expanded his kingdom and who should have gotten richer? The good people are told that money is bad, and the bad people are told that money is good, which is entirely wrong. We must recognise that earning more money is beneficial and that with increased financial resources, one can accomplish more good. One can bite into an apple to eat it, but to feed many, one must use a tool (a knife) to cut it, which represents money.

Essential money is what you must earn to stay alive and to support your family. To survive is the fundamental right of every living being on this planet. Unfortunately, for humans, we have created a system in which we have to earn to survive. With essential money comes the most significant dilemma. People who are just getting by are told that they should remain satisfied with what they have. If they choose to earn more money, they may become corrupted. More money comes with more problems. In many Eastern societies, it is often said that one can become very rich only by engaging in wrongdoing, such as cheating or gambling, and that there is no other way to attain wealth. That's not true as well. You can become wealthy by conquering your weaknesses and with sheer determination. Now more than ever, you have the opportunity to earn more money by doing the right things. By developing software, promoting a healthier lifestyle, or simply providing exceptional medical services, you can earn a substantial amount of money. However, it is not wrong to be satisfied with essential money, but you must make that choice by yourself, not under the pressure of others. People who are content with what they have tend to live longer and happier lives than those who are not. Thus, we should reflect and question: Am I satisfied with myself? Or do I want to do more good for the things around me?

Lastly, the bad money. I have heard many people say that there is no such thing as bad money. Either you have it, or you don't. In the world of social media, I am sure you must have come across influencers suggesting the power of money, why you should do everything to be rich, or how they became rich by investing in crypto currency or through betting, etc.

Could it be true? Is there no such thing as bad money? People promote gambling apps to earn money and justify it because it's legal. What happens when a country passes a law that makes killing legal? Then, one should kill others to earn money, because it is legal?

How about a salesman lying to a potential customer to sell their product? That's a prevalent thing, isn't it? Everyone does that. That's how the world works, but does it? If one can justify lying to sell a product to earn a living, then why do we all despise the scammers? There is not much difference between a lying salesman and a scammer. They are both doing the wrong things: lying, seeking to make money, and taking advantage of customers' vulnerability. The only difference is that one provides the wrong product, while the other provides nothing at all.

Now ask yourself again, is lying okay to sell? We become hypocrites depending on the situation. We have all been hypocrites at some point or another. A doctor is earning to provide for his family, and a drug dealer is also earning to provide for his family. What is the difference? They can both justify their actions by saying its essential money, but is that really the case?

Earning money is one of the most important things one can do in this world. There is no escape from it unless you were brought up to be a monk or a saint; even then, you would have to take help from people who are earning money. There is no way around it. Then why not do it with awareness? You must discard any preconceived notions about money and what others have told you about it. You have to self-examine and decide which path you want to take.

Money is not a hindrance to enlightenment or living happily. It's simply a tool that everyone has to use. However, how you choose to use it is entirely up to you.

ENDING

Ultimately, I would reiterate what I said at the beginning. Reading this book or any other will not ease your suffering. Listening to me or anyone else will not make you truly happy. Following one guru or another will not bring you fulfilment. Why? Since all anyone can do for you is provide information, some information may be more relevant than others, but that's the only difference. The one person who can genuinely make you happy, content and enlightened is you. People can only tell you about different meditation techniques, but that does not guarantee they will work for you. However, if you understand how meditation works, you may find a method that suits you best. No guru or motivational speaker can permanently alleviate your pain. However, if you understand what pain is, you may find a way to release it yourself.

If following someone or something blindly were to work, then there would only be one religion in the world. If one book had helped, there would have been no need for another.

You must ask yourself: Do you want to be a monk or a Buddha? Because many monks follow Buddha, but Buddha followed no one, he created his own path. He did not choose to follow the path he was born into. If what worked for him worked for everyone, you would see many Buddhas. But is that the case? There was only one Jesus, one Buddha, one Mahavira, and one Krishna. There can't be two. Every God you believe in chose not to believe in the God they were told to believe in. They found their own path, which led to their liberation. Similarly, you must understand everything but not follow anything. You are unique, and your circumstances are exceptional as well. What worked for me will not work for you. However, if you are willing to discover who you are, then you will. Learn from a guru, teacher, motivational speaker, scholar and more, but follow your own path. Find your own path and answers. As there is no road, there are only directions. You must build your own road to travel. If you keep searching for a road, you will be disappointed. However, if you follow the directions, you will reach your destination.

To conclude, believe in yourself, be curious about yourself, seek knowledge and know there is only you for yourself.

ABOUT THE AUTHOR

Abhishek Aggarwal has walked many paths, both external and internal, in search of meaning and understanding. With a Bachelor's and a Master's degree from Melbourne, Australia, he entered the world with knowledge and ambition, only to discover that life's most profound lessons are not taught in classrooms.

His journey took him through a multitude of roles, from managing restaurants and kitchens to overseeing construction sites, navigating the world of banking, and taking on countless odd jobs, each offering its own triumphs, challenges, and insights. Yet, despite accomplishments and outward success, he found himself facing the quiet despair of anxiety, depression, and panic attacks and a deeper question: why does life still feel incomplete when all the pieces seem to be in place?

It was amid financial, family, and personal crises that Abhishek embarked on a profound inner journey, seeking answers to life's most persistent and difficult questions. That search became Me For Myself, a book born from the raw reality of struggle, reflection, and the pursuit of understanding. Through it, he shares his observations on the mind, the heart, and the silent conflicts that shape every human life, inviting readers to confront their own shadows, question what they have been taught, and discover clarity within themselves.

Contact details:
Email: contact@abhishekaggarwalbooks.com
Website: www.abhishekaggarwalbooks.com